Praise for *Domain Storytelling*

"This book provides a wonderful introduction to an approachable, structured, narrative-based technique for collaborative domain modeling. And for those wanting to go deeper, Stefan and Henning will help you not only to avoid common facilitation pitfalls, but also to integrate the domain knowledge into your everyday development work."

—*Paul Rayner, author of* The EventStorming Handbook

"This book is destined to be the definitive resource on Domain Storytelling for many years."

—*Mike Cohn, co-founder of the Agile Alliance*

"Until now, when people talk about visualization, they usually mean 'words in boxes on a whiteboard.' Representing the user's needs and journeys has been somewhat awkward, with either long form descriptions or series of wireframes. What Stefan and Henning have achieved is a method that shows what's really happening. A Domain Storytelling model shows who's doing what with whom, in what order, and for what purpose, in a clear, truly visual way. It's easy enough to learn how to build these models, but more importantly, an uninitiated reader can understand and critique the models at first sight. That makes Domain Storytelling a powerful communication tool that I believe will become widely used in software product companies and beyond."

—*Mathias Verraes, curator of Domain-Driven Design Europe*

"This is a great addition to any Domain-Driven Design practitioner's bookshelf."

—*Julie Lerman, software coach, The Data Farm*

"All organizations are being disrupted through the rapid advance of change, and my job is to teach people how to apply the Kanban method in their business life. In that context we use Domain Storytelling while exploring and extracting value streams in organizations in a very successful way. With their book, Stefan Hofer and Henning Schwentner explain how collaboration can and does lead the way to transforming our ways of working."

—*Altuğ Bilgin Altıntaş, business agility engineer, accredited Kanban trainer & coach, author of* Kanban Metodu ile Çeviklik, *co-organizer of FlowConf*

"From a story to working software—this book helps you to get to the essence of what to build. Highly recommended!"

—*Oliver Drotbohm*

T0326628

"This book is a rare achievement, combining a pragmatic guide to a powerful domain modeling technique and a wealth of distilled insights from key aspects of Domain-Driven Design, without being a tome. The authors present a convincing case that conversational stories told and visualized in a natural language pave the fastest path to quality business software. Be prepared for fingers itching to start your own Domain Storytelling while reading the well-curated case studies."

—*Xin Yao, chief software architect at Danske Bank*

"Practicing Domain Storytelling is a journey towards deep and true understanding of the problem domain you are working on. While discovering subtle inner workings of the business, be prepared for some unexpected solutions to reveal themselves along the way. This book will put you in a position to embark on that journey on your own and will guide you along the way."

—*Mufrid Krilic, DDD and Domain Storytelling practitioner*

"Domain Storytelling served as a key bridge between our business, products, and technology stacks, and between our past to our future. Using the practice, everyone who participated—from P&L and Operations team leaders to individual engineers and product leads—levelled-up their understanding of where we intended (and needed) to take the business, aligned with each other, and understood how cross-functional product and engineering teams would function within the relevant bounded contexts that collectively represented our future business model. And many (even most!) found it a fun and liberating process.

Domain Storytelling is a practical methodology rooted in the language and context of customers and business, so accessible and valuable to cross-functions (not just engineering) within your business. I recommend the book and, more importantly, the methodology!"

—*Jim Banister, chief product officer, Raisin DS GmbH*

"As a product manager I really love visualization. Domain Storytelling was one of the techniques I met at the very beginning of my Domain-Driven Design journey (in 2017). I was impressed, amazed, and at the same time surprised in a very positive way that this is exactly what is needed by someone who facilitates the communication between development teams and business. It is very easy to learn and focuses on the pictographic language that makes it possible for literally everyone to understand and take advantage of. I would recommend using it immediately; don't think too much, just start and go with the flow! Believe me it will be worth it. :)"

—*Zsófia Herendi, product manager*

Domain Storytelling

Pearson Addison-Wesley
Signature Series

 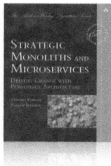  

Visit informit.com/awss/vernon **for a complete list of available publications.**

The Pearson Addison-Wesley Signature Series provides readers with practical and authoritative information on the latest trends in modern technology for computer professionals. The series is based on one simple premise: great books come from great authors.

Vaughn Vernon is a champion of simplifying software architecture and development, with an emphasis on reactive methods. He has a unique ability to teach and lead with Domain-Driven Design using lightweight tools to unveil unimagined value. He helps organizations achieve competitive advantages using enduring tools such as architectures, patterns, and approaches, and through partnerships between business stakeholders and software developers.

Vaughn's Signature Series guides readers toward advances in software development maturity and greater success with business-centric practices. The series emphasizes organic refinement with a variety of approaches—reactive, object, and functional architecture and programming; domain modeling; right-sized services; patterns; and APIs—and covers best uses of the associated underlying technologies.

Make sure to connect with us!
informit.com/socialconnect

the trusted technology learning source

Domain Storytelling

A Collaborative, Visual, and Agile Way to
Build Domain-Driven Software

Stefan Hofer
Henning Schwentner

✦Addison-Wesley

Boston • Columbus • New York • San Francisco • Amsterdam • Cape Town
Dubai • London • Madrid • Milan • Munich • Paris • Montreal • Toronto • Delhi • Mexico City
São Paulo • Sydney • Hong Kong • Seoul • Singapore • Taipei • Tokyo

For information about buying this title in bulk quantities, or for special sales opportunities (which may include electronic versions; custom cover designs; and content particular to your business, training goals, marketing focus, or branding interests), please contact our corporate sales department at corpsales@ pearsoned.com or (800) 382-3419.

For government sales inquiries, please contact governmentsales@pearsoned.com.

For questions about sales outside the U.S., please contact intlcs@pearson.com.

Visit us on the Web: informit.com/aw

Library of Congress Control Number: 2021943443

Copyright © 2022 Pearson Education, Inc.

Cover image: salajean/Shutterstock

Figure 5.6: © Henning Schwentner

Figure A.1: © Anita Krabbel

Figures A.2, A.3: © WPS – Workplace Solutions

Sunflower icon: VECTOR ICONS/Shutterstock

Checkmark and cross icons: sudowoodo/123RF

Car icon: AF studio/Shutterstock

Light bulb icon: Irina Adamovich/Shutterstock

ISBN-13: 978-0-13-745891-2
ISBN-10: 0-13-745891-6

ScoutAutomatedPrintCode

To our families.

Contents

Domain Stories

Series Editor Foreword

My signature series emphasizes organic growth and refinement, which I describe in more detail below. First, there's a story of organic growth connected with this particular book.

My book, *Implementing Domain-Driven Design*, known as "the red book," arrived at an important point in time. Prior to my red book there were only a handful of people with an accurate and thorough understanding of this advanced approach to software development—those who could be described as leaders. Related to this, few Domain-Driven Design (DDD) meetups and tools to help practitioners existed at that time. I co-founded the DDD Denver meetup in 2011, well before my red book was published in 2013, but that was one of perhaps five or so to be found anywhere. By 2021, you could find 142 Domain-Driven Design meetup groups globally, with 93,171 members, and they are still growing. When that number reached 10, and then 20, and then 25, did anyone think that they would eventually find nearly 150? As a result of this organic growth, the number of leaders and supporting tools provided for DDD also grew. Timing is everything, and I am thrilled to have contributed several catalysts at times when they were needed most, which led to the expansion of DDD. Before explaining how this book and its authors are involved in this organic growth, first consider the series that hosts it.

My signature series is designed and curated to guide readers toward advances in software development maturity and greater success with business-centric practices. The series emphasizes *organic growth and refinement* with a variety of approaches—reactive, object, as well as functional architecture and programming; domain modeling; right-sized services; patterns; and APIs—and covers best uses of the associated underlying technologies.

From here I am focusing now on only two words: *organic refinement*.

The first word, *organic*, stood out to me recently when a friend and colleague used it to describe software architecture. I have heard and used the word *organic* in connection with software development, but I didn't think about that word as carefully as I did then when I personally consumed the two used together: *organic architecture*.

Think about the word *organic*, and even the word *organism*. For the most part these are used when referring to living things, but they are also used to describe inanimate things that feature some characteristics that resemble life-forms. *Organic* originates in Greek. Its etymology is with reference to a functioning organ of the body. If you read the etymology of *organ*, it has a broader use, and in fact organic followed suit: body organs, to implement, describes a tool for making or doing, a musical instrument.

We can readily think of numerous organic objects—living organisms—from the very large to the microscopic single-celled life-forms. With the second use of organism, though, examples may not as readily pop into our mind. One example is an organization, which includes the prefix of both *organic* and *organism*. In this use of *organism*, I'm describing something that is structured with bidirectional dependencies. An organization is an organism because it has organized parts. This kind of organism cannot survive without the parts, and the parts cannot survive without the organism.

Taking that perspective, we can continue applying this thinking to nonliving things because they exhibit characteristics of living organisms. Consider the atom. Every single atom is a system unto itself, and all living things are composed of atoms. Yet, atoms are inorganic and do not reproduce. Even so, it's not difficult to think of atoms as living things in the sense that they are endlessly moving, functioning. Atoms even bond with other atoms. When this occurs, each atom is not only a single system unto itself, but also becomes a subsystem along with other atoms as subsystems, with their combined behaviors yielding a greater whole system.

So then, all kinds of concepts regarding software are quite organic in that nonliving things are still "characterized" by aspects of living organisms. When we discuss software model concepts using concrete scenarios, or draw an architecture diagram, or write a unit test and its corresponding domain model unit, software starts to come alive. It isn't static, because we continue to discuss how to make it better, subjecting it to refinement, where one scenario leads to another, and that has an impact on the architecture and the domain model. As we continue to iterate, the increasing value in refinements leads to incremental growth of the organism. As time progresses so does the software. We wrangle with and tackle complexity through useful abstractions, and the software grows and changes shapes, all with the explicit purpose of making work better for real living organisms at global scales.

Sadly, software organics tend to grow poorly more often than they grow well. Even if they start out life in good health, they tend to get diseases, become deformed, grow unnatural appendages, atrophy, and deteriorate. Worse still is that these symptoms are caused by efforts to refine the software that go wrong instead of making things better. The worst part is that with every failed refinement, everything that goes wrong with these complexly ill bodies doesn't cause their death. (Oh, if they could just die!) Instead, we have to kill them and killing them requires nerves, skills, and the intestinal fortitude of a dragon slayer. No, not one, but dozens of vigorous dragon slayers. Actually, make that dozens of dragon slayers who have really big brains.

That's where this series comes into play. I am curating a series designed to help you mature and reach greater success with a variety of approaches—reactive, object, and functional architecture and programming; domain modeling; right-sized services; patterns; and APIs. And along with that, the series covers best uses of the associated underlying technologies. It's not accomplished at one fell swoop. It requires organic refinement with purpose and skill. I and the other authors are here to help. To that end, we've delivered our very best to achieve our goal.

That's why I chose this book, *Domain Storytelling*, to be among mine and others in my series. The previously noted organic expansion of DDD has resulted in new practitioners and leaders, as well as innovation in tools that support it. Collaborative modeling with this brilliant tool enables visual exploration while simultaneously capturing domain-driven discoveries and model usage scenarios with vital clarity that leads to increased success. Domain Storytelling should not be viewed as a replacement for previous tools, but an opportunity to gain a greater variety of instruments of knowledge acquisition. Novel and more challenging modeling situations call for an array of useful tools that can be employed together.

With this new book, Stefan Hofer and Henning Schwentner are establishing themselves as two of the new leaders. They have brought us an additional tool in Domain Storytelling, to be used for wrangling with greater complexities that we face today and will continue to face over the years ahead. That's organic.

—*Vaughn Vernon, series editor*

Foreword

In 2004, Eric Evans published *Domain-Driven Design*, a timeless book that has become an all-time classic in software engineering literature. Evans projected his vision of software developers as people who collaborated closely with subject matter experts to iteratively solve domain-related problems for users. At the time, this was heresy against mainstream practices oriented around data models, big up-front planning, and programmers as mere order-takers.

Evans's text was a masterpiece, but still it was missing something. For a decade, DDD was perceived by the mainstream as a few programming patterns and became synonymous with over-engineering. Evans's book spoke frequently about domain experts and technical experts crunching domain knowledge together, but it didn't give readers enough practical guidance in the same way it did for the technical DDD patterns.

The mid-2010s saw a DDD renaissance, which continues to this day. Vaughn Vernon's book *Implementing Domain-Driven Design* was pivotal in correcting many misconceptions and making DDD more approachable. And a new generation of practitioners led by Alberto Brandolini, including Stefan and Henning, emphatically added the missing piece of the DDD puzzle by introducing new collaborative modeling techniques into the community. The mainstream perception of DDD is now just as much sticky notes on the wall as it is programming design patterns. Evans's 2004 prophecy is truly now a reality.

Domain Storytelling stands out for its pictographic, structured, and scenario-based nature. But this book is far more than a guide to Domain Storytelling. Stefan and Henning are passionate, intelligent, and experienced collaborative domain modelers. This book takes you into their brains through their thinking patterns and deep into the principles of collaborative domain modeling and workshop facilitation. This work provides insights that will be useful regardless of the technique you decide to use and regardless of how much you know about DDD. It may even inspire you to invent the next generation of collaborative modeling techniques.

I've had the chance to meet Stefan and Henning at numerous conferences. But one sticks out in my memory more than others: Explore DDD 2018 in Denver. Their enthusiasm for Domain Storytelling captivated the audience (including me) in a talk where they presented a case study of using Domain Storytelling to build systems that prevent ships getting stranded in the port of Hamburg. Their role play with props was the icing on the cake. I also got to attend their hands-on Domain Storytelling workshop where their pure love of the game shone through and had attendees (including me) excitedly modeling the cinema experience.

I also have fond recollections of the night before the main conference. Eric Evans gave an evening keynote to officially kick off Explore DDD, and I was with Stefan and Henning at the social event afterwards. They made an effort to help conference attendees feel included by inviting them into discussions and striking up conversations, and they made us all belly laugh with their clever humor.

I hope this book provides you with the inspiration, enthusiasm, and smiles that Stefan and Henning have brought to me and many others.

—Nick Tune

Preface

Misunderstandings between software developers and people from the business departments are a common problem. Bad communication is a plague that makes projects fail. Domain Storytelling is a remedy because this technique transforms domain knowledge into effective business software. Domain Storytelling brings together domain experts, software developers, user experience designers, product owners, product managers, and business analysts on the same page. They learn from each other by telling stories and drawing them as easy-to-understand pictures.

Who Should Read This Book

The book is aimed at everyone involved or interested in software development, including nontechnical readers. There are only a few code examples, and, generally speaking, no prior knowledge is required. Where it makes sense, we point you to some recommended reading.

Beyond software development professionals, the book is also relevant to CxOs, executives, directors, team leads from business departments, and domain experts. They can use the book to improve their understanding of their business processes and to improve communication with their IT counterparts.

This Book in the Software Development Landscape

This book is meant to be a practical guide. We wanted to keep it concise, although we were tempted to write a book on Domain-Driven Design, domain modeling, requirements, agile, and software development in general. All of these topics are relevant to Domain Storytelling and are referenced in this book, but we tried not to dive too deep into topics that other authors have already addressed brilliantly. If you are curious, here is an (incomplete) list of authors who have influenced us:

- **Heinz Züllighoven et al.:** The *Tools and Material Approach* [Züllighoven 2004] is important for how we look at software development. It promotes user-centric software development and is built around the powerful metaphors *tool* and *material*. The book was first published in the late 1990s and covers topics such as iterative-incremental development, modeling, scenarios, and patterns for software construction.

- **Eric Evans:** *Domain-Driven Design (DDD)* [Evans 2004] shares many characteristics with the Tools and Material Approach, although the two were developed independently from each other. The concepts *bounded context* and *ubiquitous language* immediately resonated with us. DDD opened a new area of application for Domain Storytelling, influencing the direction in which we have been pushing the method in the last couple of years.

- **Kent Beck et al.:** The *Agile Manifesto* [Beck et al. 2001] put "individuals and interactions over processes and tools" and "working software over comprehensive documentation." Domain Storytelling is about individuals and their interactions on two levels: (1) domain stories show people and their collaboration, and (2) the workshop in which these stories are told brings together humans to interact with each other. *Extreme Programming (XP)* brought the concept of stories into software development and introduced *user stories* to the agile world [Beck 1999, Beck/Andres 2004, and Cohn 2004].

- **Alistair Cockburn:** *Writing Effective Use Cases* [Cockburn 2001] is one of our favorite books on requirements. Even if you do not apply use cases, the book is worth a read. It shows how to follow an agile path from domain to software. We borrowed the idea of *goal levels* and applied it to Domain Storytelling.

- **Gojko Adzic:** *Specification by Example* [Adzic 2011] highlights the importance of conversations in software development. We started to view software development as a series of conversations about the domain and requirements, supported by several "conversation methods" like Domain Storytelling. We share Adzic's views on requirements and the benefits of using examples.

- **Christiane Floyd:** We had the pleasure of learning from Professor Floyd at the University of Hamburg. She researched and taught (among other things) modeling theory, the limits of modeling, sociotechnical aspects of modeling and software development, and participatory design. She published papers in German and English. If you are curious, see for example "Software Development as Reality Construction" [Floyd 1992] and search for papers on her *STEPS* approach, an early example of what later became known as agile software development.

What This Book Covers

This book is divided into two parts: Part I explains the method, and Part II describes how to use and adapt it for specific purposes.

Part I, "Domain Storytelling Explained": This part of the book contains everything you need to know to use Domain Storytelling for learning about a domain.

Chapter 1, "Introduction": This chapter explains what Domain Storytelling actually is. Also, we introduce a case study that will give you a first impression of the method and show you why it is useful.

Chapter 2, "The Pictographic Language": This chapter describes the graphical notation. To record domain stories visually, you need a set of symbols and rules for combining them. This chapter will also show you what we consider good language style and what pitfalls to avoid. If you have never tried Domain Storytelling, you should do so after finishing Chapter 2. Get out a piece of paper and a pen, and model a workflow that you are familiar with. However, before trying Domain Storytelling in a workshop situation, you should continue reading the rest of Part I.

Chapter 3, "Scenario-Based Modeling": This chapter introduces you to one of the major differences between domain stories and other business process modeling languages: Every domain story is about one case. You will learn which cases you should model and how to keep an overview.

Chapter 4, "Scope": This chapter is about the level of detail that stories have, whether they are descriptive or exploratory, and the amount of technical information they contain. You will need to consider all these factors every time you start a new domain story. This chapter will help you to choose the right scope.

Chapter 5, "Modeling Tools": This summarizes our experience with different modeling tools. We recommend which tools are useful in which situations, describe their strengths and weaknesses, and give practical tips that will help you model more effortlessly.

Chapter 6, "The Workshop Format": This chapter shows that Domain Storytelling works best when used for collaborative modeling. You will learn how to prepare, conduct, and follow up on a workshop. This chapter will help you to become a good moderator.

Chapter 7, "Relationship to Other Modeling Methods": This chapter discusses other modeling methods and workshop formats and how to combine Domain Storytelling with them. This chapter will help you to pick the right tool for the right job.

Part II, "Purposes": This part of the book deals with the different problems and purposes for which Domain Storytelling can be used. Even though we use the same example in all chapters of Part II, you do not have to read the chapters in order. Just pick the purposes that you are interested in.

Chapter 8, "Case Study—Alphorn Auto Leasing Inc.": This chapter introduces a second, more comprehensive case study.

Chapter 9, "Learning Domain Language": Speaking the language of the domain experts is the key for effective conversations about business processes and software requirements. This chapter is for you if you are new to a domain, if the software that you work on does not use real terms from the domain and you want to change that, or if you work in an organization where no real domain language exists and you want one to emerge.

Chapter 10, "Finding Boundaries": Many domains are too big to be understood and modeled as a whole. You need to break down a domain into manageable units. Read this chapter if you are struggling with a monolith and want to reorganize it or split it into more manageable parts, if you want to design microservices, or if you want to apply Domain-Driven Design and have difficulties identifying bounded contexts. The chapter will also help if your development team has become too big to work efficiently or if you already have more than one development team and want to find out how you can organize the work for these teams.

Chapter 11, "Working with Requirements": How do you bridge the gap between domain knowledge and requirements? We show you how to derive requirements from domain stories so that you can discuss priorities and viable products. This chapter is for you if you consider yourself a product owner, product manager, business analyst, requirements engineer, or developer in a cross-functional team that does its own requirements analysis.

Chapter 12, "Modeling in Code": If your ultimate goal is to develop software, then, at some point, you need to move from modeling with diagrams and sticky notes to modeling in programming languages. This chapter will show you how to transition from visual modeling to code.

Chapter 13, "Supporting Organizational Change": The goal of a new software system usually is to make work easier, faster, and more efficient (in short: better). This goal will not be reached by digitalizing bad manual processes. Neither will a pile of requirements magically turn into a seamless business workflow. To build good business software, you need to go beyond merely modeling the current situation. You will need to design the future way of working. Domain stories help to do this and visualize how new software will change the way people work. Read this chapter if you want to optimize business processes, roll out new software, or discuss and promote change in business processes.

Chapter 14, "Deciding Make or Buy and Choosing Off-the-Shelf Software": Not every piece of software is custom-built. Many domains are supported by off-the-shelf software. Domain stories can help to decide if a new software system should be developed or bought. If the decision is to buy an existing solution, usually several vendors will offer their products. Here too, domain stories can be useful in making a decision.

Chapter 15, "Finding Shadow IT": When you are trying to consolidate software application landscapes or promote digitalization, shadow IT stands in your way. Every company beyond a certain size uses software that the central IT department is not aware of. All those little solutions that run in business departments and that hardly anyone knows about are often business-critical. Domain experts use shadow IT unconsciously, so it is easily overlooked. Domain stories can help IT and management find this shadow IT and see the whole IT landscape.

Chapter 16, "Conclusion": We take a look into the future of Domain Storytelling and sum up its essence.

Conventions

When we define a new term, we set it in bold, e.g., **actor**. Terms that were defined by other authors are set in italics when we use them for the first time, e.g., *bounded context*. Scope factors appear in small caps, e.g., COARSE-GRAINED. Words from case studies are surrounded by quotation marks, like "moviegoer." Code is set in constant width, like the class MovieTicket.

Important notes are marked with a lightbulb icon: 🔅. When we give concrete advice, our tips are marked with a checkmark icon: ✅.

We provide examples in the form of case studies and "stories from the trenches." Appearances of case study Alphorn Auto Leasing Inc. are indicated with a car icon: 🚗. The stories from the trenches are marked with a sunflower icon: ✸.

Legend for "Opening Stories"

As modelers, we couldn't resist the temptation to describe Domain Storytelling itself with domain stories. That's why several chapters of this book begin with an "opening story"—a short domain story that explains what the chapter is about. The legend in Table P.1 will help you to interpret the icons that we use in those stories.

Table P.1 *Icons used in "Opening Stories"*

Icon	Meaning
	A domain story as a diagram
	Any other kind of diagram
	Building blocks of a domain story diagram
	Activities of a domain story diagram
	A text such as a user story or a source code file, etc.

Supplementary Materials

On www.domainstorytelling.org/book, we created a companion website for this book [DomainStorytelling BookWebsite]. It contains the example domain stories that we show in this book. The examples were created with Egon.io, an open-source modeling tool that our company WPS – Workplace Solutions created [Egon.io Website]. You can import the source files from this book into Egon.io and "replay" the domain stories (instructions are on the website).

The companion website also contains the bibliography of this book, with clickable links to online resources.

Furthermore, on www.domainstorytelling.org, you will find links to useful materials, including a collection of videos and articles [DomainStorytelling Website].

About the Cover

The covers of the books in Vaughn Vernon's Signature Series all use images that have an organic theme. We were happy about this because domain stories develop in an organic way, too. Like the sunflowers you see on the cover, a domain story starts from a small seed, grows, and if everything goes well, eventually blooms into a beautiful blossom. The relationship of domain and domain story is similar to the one between sun and sunflower:

- A sunflower can't exist without sun. Likewise, a domain story will dry up without contact to the domain.

- The sunflower looks like the sun. Likewise, the domain story is formed to resemble the domain.

- During the day, the sunflower turns its head to follow the sun. Likewise, the domain story follows the domain.

- A sunflower often lives in a field together with many other sunflowers. Likewise, a domain story usually doesn't come alone but together with other stories.

All these properties make the sunflower not only a splendid cover picture plant but also a friendly-looking symbol for Domain Storytelling.

With that out of the way, welcome to The Sunflower Book. We wish you happy reading and happy modeling!

Acknowledgments

Many people have encouraged us to write this book and helped us improve it by giving valuable feedback. We would like to thank all of you!

We thank our friends and colleagues for sharing their experience and stories with us, especially (and in alphabetic order) Jörn Koch, Dorota Kochanowska, Carola Lilienthal, Carsten Lill, Kai Rüstmann, Martin Schimak, and Heinz Züllighoven. Heinz deserves an especially big, big *thank you* for his endless support. Isabella Tran and Samaneh Javanbakht helped us with their language skills.

Carola Lilienthal and Guido Gryczan, CEOs of WPS – Workplace Solutions GmbH, have been our managers for more than a decade and a half now. Their continued support made Domain Storytelling possible in the first place.

Despite coining the name and writing the first book about it, we did not invent Domain Storytelling. Rather, it emerged organically out of another modeling method. The seed was planted in the 1990s at the University of Hamburg, and many people have helped to cultivate it. They deserve credit and our gratitude. That is why we dedicated the appendix, "The History of Domain Storytelling," to them.

An earlier version of this book was first published as an e-book on Leanpub, a self-publishing platform. We thank everyone who downloaded our book. Every download increased our confidence and motivated us to turn our original ~40-page booklet into a proper book. We appreciate the useful tips that Cyrille Martraire gave us when we transitioned to Pearson.

This book could not have been written without the power of open-source software. Pandoc and Perl enabled us to write the source in Markdown. We used Inkscape and Draw.io for many illustrations. A hearty thank-you to the authors of these great tools.

We thank Altuğ Bilgin Altıntaş, Jim Banister, Mike Cohn, Oliver Drotbohm, Zsófia Herendi, Mufrid Krilic, Julie Lerman, Paul Rayner, Mathias Verraes, and Xin Yao for contributing endorsements for our book. They represent several software communities that we care about deeply. The community of Domain-Driven Design practitioners has been crucial to the success of Domain Storytelling. We want to thank all the kind and welcoming organizers of conferences and meetups for giving us a platform to discuss our ideas—especially Mathias Verraes for giving us a first international stage at DDD Europe and for producing a printed Domain Storytelling booklet with us.

We are grateful for the trust that Vaughn Vernon has put in us. Being part of his *Addison-Wesley Signature Series* is an honor. Nick Tune wrote an awesome foreword, both inspiring and personal. We hope that our paths will cross many times in the future, like they did in Denver in 2018.

Writing a text is one thing, but making a book out of it is another. That's why we would like to thank the people at Pearson we've had the pleasure to work with. Our executive editor Haze Humbert and content producer Julie Nahil guided us competently through the development and production process. Development editor Adriana Cloud improved the flow and clarity of our text while preserving our voice. Matt Takane provided us with a very helpful review. Copy editor Kim Wimpsett patiently endured our stubbornness and fine-tuned our text. The book was composed by Aswini Kumar and her team.

Writing this book took a lot of time—uncounted evenings and weekends that our loved ones had to spend without us. Stefan sends gratitude and love to his wife, Samaneh. Henning sends gratitude and love to his children, Lennart, Joris, Friedo, Tara, and Aurelia, and to his partner, Julia. Dear families, we thank you for your patience, understanding, and support!

About the Authors

Stefan Hofer is bad at drawing. However, he thinks he can build up domain knowledge by drawing domain stories. Stefan studied software engineering in Austria and earned a PhD in computer science. Since 2005, he has been working for WPS – Workplace Solutions in Hamburg, Germany. His job there is to help teams develop software that does the right job the right way. He maintains domainstorytelling.org. You can reach him on Twitter (@hofstef) or by email to stefan@domainstorytelling.org.

Henning Schwentner is a programmer who has been into computers ever since he got an Amiga 500 in the early 90s. He was lucky enough to turn this passion into a profession and works as a coder, coach, and consultant at WPS – Workplace Solutions. He helps teams to bring structure into their existing software or to build new systems with a sustainable architecture from scratch. Henning is the author of LeasingNinja.io, the German translator of *Domain-Driven Design Distilled*, and co-organizer of CoMoCamp. He tweets as @hschwentner and reads emails addressed to henning@domainstorytelling.org. Henning is the proud father of five children in a very special patchwork situation.

Part I

Domain Storytelling Explained

This part covers everything you need to know to get started. You will learn the following:

- Why Domain Storytelling is useful to organizations, business experts, and development teams
- How to prepare and run workshops in which domain stories are discussed and modeled visually
- How to choose which examples to use for domain stories (and how to deal with everything else that could happen)
- How to decide on the level of detail and other properties of a domain story
- Which options in modeling tools you have
- How to combine Domain Storytelling with other methods and when to choose one over the other

After reading this part and some practice, you will be prepared to moderate Domain Storytelling workshops.

Chapter 1

Introduction

Spoken language is deeply, deeply human. Some things must be said that cannot be written.

—Avraham Poupko [Poupko 2018]

What Is Domain Storytelling?

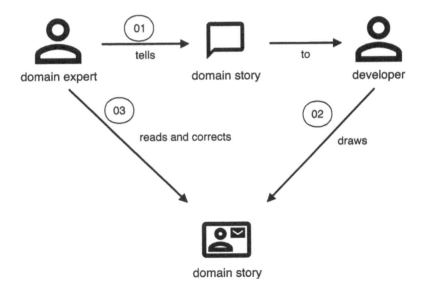

Domain Storytelling is a collaborative modeling technique that highlights how people work together. Its primary purpose is to transform domain knowledge into business software. This purpose is achieved by bringing together people from different backgrounds and allowing them to learn from each other by telling and visualizing stories.

Telling stories is a basic form of human communication. It is deeply rooted in all of us since the times our ancestors lived in caves.[1] In our modern world, telling a story might seem archaic or childish. How can an activity so informal help us to build business-critical software for domains such as logistics, car manufacturing, e-commerce, and banking?

We believe that conversations cannot be adequately replaced by written, formal specifications. Attempts to do so have even widened the gap between business and software development. But that is not just our personal opinion. Consider software development approaches like *agile*, *Domain-Driven Design*, or *Behavior-Driven Development*. These philosophies focus on feedback and stakeholder involvement. Nevertheless, making great business software is hard, but rarely is this because of technical problems. So why then? Because software developers need to understand how the day-to-day business operates. They need to become domain experts themselves—not for the whole domain but at least for the part they build software for. As Alberto Brandolini put it:

> It's developer's (mis)understanding, not expert knowledge, that gets released in production. [Brandolini 2016]

Telling stories still works in the age of software. In our experience, telling and listening to stories helps with the following:

- Understanding a domain
- Establishing a shared language between domain experts and IT experts
- Overcoming misunderstandings
- Clarifying software requirements
- Implementing the right software
- Structuring that software
- Designing viable, software-supported business processes

Telling stories is a means for transporting domain knowledge from the heads of domain experts into the heads of developers, testers, product owners, product

---

1. See *The Desirability of Storytellers* [Yong 2017].

managers, business analysts—anyone who is involved in developing software. Of course, we do not sit around campfires in dark and damp caves anymore. We share our stories while we meet in front of a whiteboard in a workshop. The domain experts are our storytellers. We want them to tell us the true stories from the trenches—no abstract "ifs," no hypothetical "coulds." We want concrete and real examples of what actually happens in the domain. We want *domain stories*.

> You can learn more from a good example than from a bad abstraction.

Once, storytelling was an oral activity. Domain Storytelling is an oral *and* visual activity, a form of *modeling*: While the domain experts tell their story in spoken language, one of the workshop's participants—the moderator—records the story as a diagram made of simple icons, arrows, and text. This way the participants get another representation of the story, which helps to uncover misunderstandings, contradictions, and plot holes. All participants see how the visual recording evolves together with the story. This makes it easy to give feedback and to contribute.

And that is Domain Storytelling.

Your First Domain Story

Matthew runs a small movie theater for arthouse films—called Metropolis—that enjoys an excellent reputation among cineastes. Local craft beer and organic snacks round off the cinema experience. One day Matthew meets his school friend Anna. When he learns that Anna has been developing apps for almost ten years, he gets an idea.

> *Movie theater manager Matthew*: "My customers like the old-fashioned charm of my cinema. But they do not like my old-fashioned box office. Today's moviegoers are not used to buying tickets in person at the box office anymore. Customers have been asking me to sell tickets online. Can you develop an app for me?"

> *App developer Anna*: "You run just one cinema, and there's only a handful of movies per week, two or three shows a day. Sounds easy."

> *Matthew*: "Great! But one small thing: We also show international movies in foreign languages in our program. Also, in addition to the online sales through

the app, I still need the box office for less tech-savvy moviegoers. And I'd like users of the app to be able to sign up for a yearly subscription."

Anna: "Subscriptions? Online and offline sales? Shows in foreign languages? That's more complicated than I thought...."

The Workshop Begins

The next day they meet again in Matthew's office. They are standing in front of a whiteboard, and Anna is holding a marker in her hand.

App developer Anna: "Yesterday you said that the app essentially has three use cases: One: selling standard tickets; two: selling special tickets for foreign-language movies; and three: signing up for a yearly subscription."

Movie theater manager Matthew: "Uh, yes, that's right."

Anna: "I would like to understand how Metropolis operates today. That will help me to develop an app that meets your requirements. Could you please explain to me how you sell tickets at the box office?"

Matthew: "Sure. You sell the tickets and mark the seat in the seating plan and...."

Anna: "Wait a minute. Who sells the tickets?"

Matthew: "I have two students working for me. But sometimes I do it myself."

Anna: "Okay, but what role do you or the students have then?"

Matthew: "Cashier."

Anna draws a stick figure on the whiteboard and writes "cashier" underneath (see Figure 1.1).

cashier

Figure 1.1 *The first actor*

Anna: "Who buys the tickets?"

Matthew: "A moviegoer. One without a subscription."

Anna draws a second stick figure and calls it "moviegoer." Next to it, she writes down that the moviegoer has no subscription (see Figure 1.2).

Figure 1.2 *The second actor and the first annotation*

Anna: "What does a moviegoer have to do to buy a ticket?"

Matthew: "They tell the cashier which show they want to see."

Anna: "I will draw a speech bubble as an icon for the show here, because the two of them talk to each other."

Anna continues drawing and numbers the arrow (see Figure 1.3).

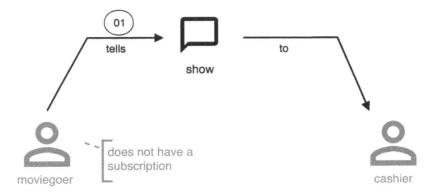

Figure 1.3 *The first activity*

Anna: "And then?"

Matthew: "Usually the cashier suggests the best seat available."

Anna: "Ah, so the moviegoer picks a seat in advance! How does the cashier suggest seats?"

Matthew: "I take the seating plan for the show and search for available seats. In the seating plan, I can see which seats have already been sold and which are still available."

Anna draws and explains the icons.

Anna: "Here, I'm using a film icon instead of the speech bubble to symbolize the show."

Matthew: "The seating plan is a grid. Can you draw a grid?" (See Figure 1.4.)

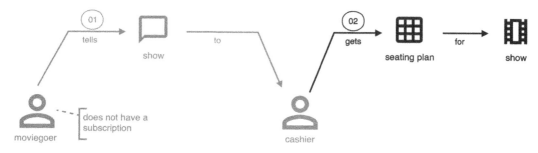

Figure 1.4 *The second activity*

Then, Anna reads back what she has understood.

Anna: "Second, the cashier gets the seating plan for the show. Third, they search for available seats. Is that OK?" (See Figure 1.5.)

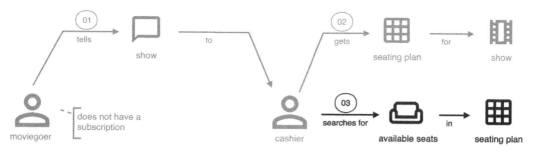

Figure 1.5 *The third activity*

Matthew nods in agreement.

Anna: "And now the cashier suggests the available seats to the moviegoer?"

Matthew: "Exactly."

Anna: "I will move the annotation 'does not have a subscription' up a bit to get enough space for that fourth sentence." (See Figure 1.6.)

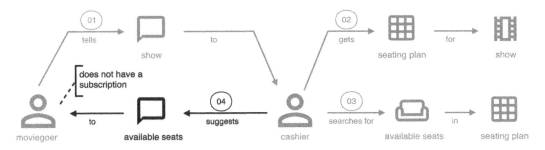

Figure 1.6 *The fourth activity*

The discussion continues….

Retelling the Story

Within a few minutes, the whiteboard is filled with a story about a moviegoer who buys tickets from a cashier at the box office. Icons and arrows are rearranged during the session. Finally, Anna retells the story from the beginning (see Figure 1.7).

> *Matthew*: "Yes, that's right. But I forgot about the international movies."

> *Anna*: "You mean the shows in a foreign language? I thought you sell special tickets for those."

> *Matthew*: "No, no! We usually show the movies in English. When it is a foreign movie, we also show it in its original language. We don't sell extra tickets; you only have to point out to the moviegoers which language the movie will be shown in."

> *Anna*: "When does the cashier do that?"

> *Matthew*: "Here."

Matthew points to the arrow with the number 4. Anna amends the sentence "Cashier suggests available seats to moviegoer" with a comment "and mentions language" (see Figure 1.8).

> *Anna*: "It seems we are finished with our little 'Going to the movies' story. Of course, we have looked only at the best possible outcome; I call this the 'happy path.' I will ask you about other cases later."

> *Matthew*: "OK."

Since Matthew does not have any further remarks, Anna takes a picture of the whiteboard with her smartphone and moves on.

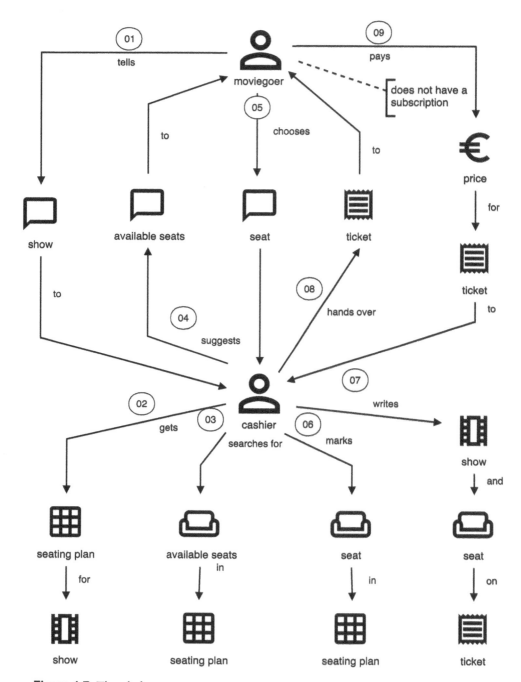

Figure 1.7 *The whole story*

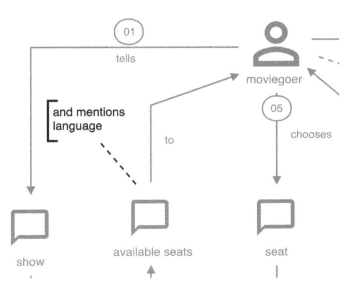

Figure 1.8 *Adding another annotation*

Exploring Further

Anna: "Once a moviegoer has bought a ticket, what do they do with it?"

Matthew: "They go to the entrance of the theater where the usher is waiting and...."

Anna turns the whiteboard around, and Matthew tells her how the usher checks tickets.

After a few FINE-GRAINED Metropolis domain stories, Anna has gained a good insight into the cinema domain. She knows terms like "seating plan," "show," "cashier," "to search for available seats," and "to mark seats." She has an initial understanding of the most important processes.

Anna realizes that it would be helpful to have an overview of the processes—a "big picture" that holds all the stories together. Anna and Matthew decide to model a COARSE-GRAINED "Going to the movies" story (see Figure 1.9).

With the knowledge about the purpose of the app and its context, she can think about how the app will work and how the processes will change.

Summary and Outlook

This section was called "Your First Domain Story"; what you have probably noticed is that this was also your first Domain Storytelling workshop.

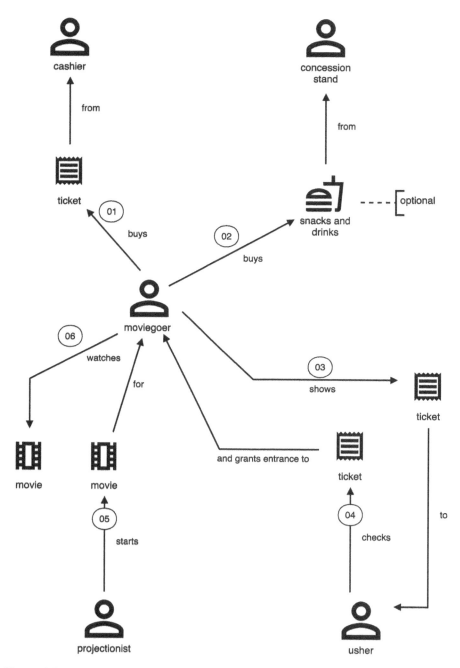

Figure 1.9 *Metropolis 1: Going to the movies—COARSE-GRAINED*

For Anna, this was surely not the first time she applied Domain Storytelling. Why was this technique useful for Anna in this situation? First, Matthew was not able to explain to her what he wanted. He had an idea in his head but had not really thought about how to make it actionable. To start a conversation about Matthew's idea, Anna first had to establish common ground: Which terms does Matthew use when he talks about his business, and what do they mean? Which business processes are relevant, and what are the important steps in those processes? Who is involved in those processes?

From that starting point, they will be able to discuss what's in scope of the project and what's not. Without Domain Storytelling, they likely would have misunderstood each other. For example, Anna initially thought that selling tickets for foreign language movies is a separate process.

Since we will refer to the Metropolis example in the following chapters, we will give the domain stories the names "Metropolis 1" (see Figure 1.9) and "Metropolis 2" (see Figure 1.10) for easier reference.

We want to highlight a few points that came up in this first example:

- Even with just a few domain stories, you can learn a lot about a domain, its language, and its business processes.
- Domain stories use a simple pictographic language to show people, their activities, and their interactions. This helps to uncover hidden assumptions and misunderstandings.
- While a domain story is told, its picture will evolve and change accordingly.
- It's not just about drawing a nice picture; it's also about bringing people together.
- Domain stories can vary in granularity.
- Usually, you will model more than one story in a workshop.
- A domain story has no "ifs" and "ors." Instead, you model only the most important alternatives—each one as a separate domain story.
- A simple whiteboard is a good enough tool for drawing domain stories.

We will cover all these points in detail in the following chapters. The first point we will discuss is the pictographic language.

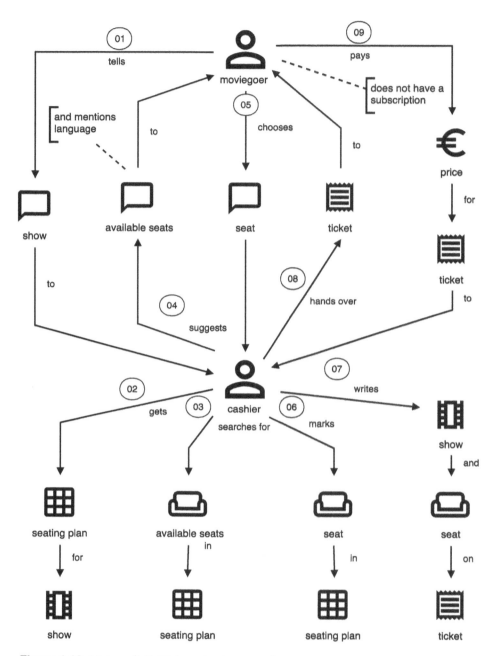

Figure 1.10 *Metropolis 2: Ticket sales, happy path*—FINE-GRAINED

Chapter 2

The Pictographic Language

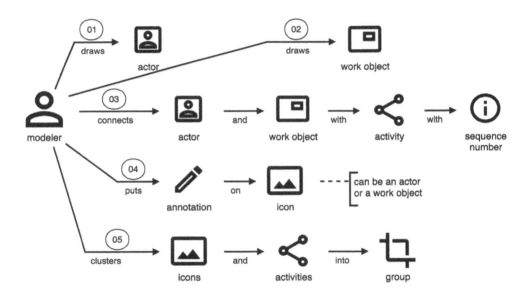

Domain Storytelling combines a pictographic language with a workshop format. While each has value on its own, it is their combination that makes Domain Storytelling work so well. We will start with the graphical notation here. To record domain stories visually, you need a set of **building blocks** (i.e., symbols[1]) and rules for combining them. The symbols consist of icons, arrows, and text.

---

1. We use the term *symbol* here with its linguistic meaning—a language is written down with symbols. The term *icon* will be used with the meaning of pictogram or image.

Actors

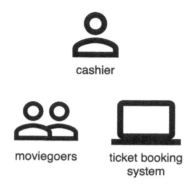

Figure 2.1 *Typical actors*

Domain stories are told from an **actor**'s perspective. An actor can be a *person* (in Figure 2.1, for example, "cashier"), a group of *people* ("moviegoers"), or a *software system* ("ticket booking system"). We use different icons to represent those different kinds of actors. What actors have in common is that they play an active role in the domain story.

The icons are all labeled with a term from the domain language. Note that we usually label actors with their role or function (e.g., "cashier") rather than a person's name (e.g., not "Matthew"). However, in some situations you may find it useful to make an exception to that rule and use concrete persons or *personas* [Cooper 1999] as actors (see also Chapter 6, "The Workshop Format").

Work Objects

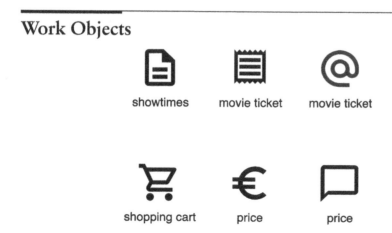

Figure 2.2 *Typical work objects. Note: "movie ticket" and "price" each appear twice with different icons*

Actors create, work with, and exchange **work objects** (see Figure 2.2) such as *documents*, *physical things*, and *digital objects*. They also exchange *information about* work objects. The pictographic language does not distinguish between work objects and information. Hence, an icon can represent all of the following:

- The actual work object itself, e.g., a movie ticket printed on a slip of paper
- A virtual representation of the work object, e.g., a digital movie ticket created by a software system
- The medium through which information about the work object is exchanged, e.g., a phone call to buy a movie ticket

Like actors, the work objects are labeled with a term from the domain language (like "showtimes," "movie ticket," etc., in Figure 2.2). Note that a work object can have different icons *within* the same domain story if the medium changes. For example, a moviegoer could receive their movie ticket via email and print it at home—the same ticket is represented with two different icons.

Icons for Actors and Work Objects

For the examples in this book, we use icon sets made up of Google's Material icons [MaterialIcons Website]. An icon set should be adapted to the domain that you want to model. For example, if you work in logistics, where shipping containers are an important work object, you should use a container icon in your domain stories. The same is true for actors—ships, cars, smartphones, etc., can all be actors, depending on your domain. Figure 2.3 shows the icon set for Metropolis.

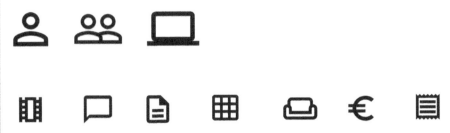

Figure 2.3 *Icons from the cinema domain*

You will see another example for an icon set when we introduce a second case study from a different domain in Part II (see Chapter 8, "Case Study— Alphorn Auto Leasing Inc.").

The icons should help with creating a clean visual. When you put together your own set of icons, keep the following in mind:

- Make sure the icons are distinct enough and simple.

- Using too many different icons will water down your pictographic language.

- The icons should convey meaning and make the domain story more tangible.

- Depending on the context, the concepts of a domain can be modeled as actors *or* work objects. At Metropolis, for example, a moviegoer's smartphone could serve as a wallet for digital tickets. Then the smartphone is modeled as a work object. Also, the new Metropolis app on a user's smartphone could notify moviegoers about cancellations. In that story, the smartphone is modeled as an actor.

Activities

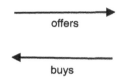

Figure 2.4 *Typical activities*

The actors' **activities** (see Figure 2.4) are shown as *arrows* and labeled with verbs from the domain language (e.g., "offers," "buys," "recommends"). Note: Actors and work objects are nouns, and activities are verbs.

Sequence Numbers

Figure 2.5 *Typical sequence numbers*

To tell a story, you need more than one sentence. Since stories are told one sentence after the other, the sentences can be brought into an order by numbering them. We usually number the sentences by adding a **sequence number** (see Figure 2.5) to the origin of the arrow that represents an activity (the predicate of a sentence).

Sequence numbers express *time* within domain stories.

In most cases, we number the activities consecutively, which means we use every number exactly once. Sometimes it makes sense to express that activities happen concurrently. If that is the case, we label the parallel activities with the same number. We recommend using this special case sparingly because it makes the sentences harder to read and weakens the story. If possible, agree on an exemplary order and use parallel activities only if it is really important for the story.

An exception to this rule is when people work together on a single work object. Then both arrows carry the same number.

We number a sentence while modeling it (as opposed to numbering all sentences at the end of modeling). This makes it easier to keep track of the story. However, the domain experts do not always get the sequence right the first time. Sometimes, sentences need to be inserted afterward, or the sequence has to be changed. Then, the sentences need to be renumbered.

Annotations

Figure 2.6 *Typical annotations*

The pictographic sentences are complemented by textual **annotations** (see Figure 2.6). Where necessary, we annotate information about variations (other cases, optional activities, possible errors). Also, it can be useful to annotate the goal of an activity (see also Chapter 6, "The Workshop Format"). We use annotations to explain terms from the domain language and to document assumptions or anything else that is noteworthy. Annotations usually concern one of the following:

- An actor, work object, or activity
- A whole sentence or several sentences
- The domain story as a whole

Annotations that concern the whole domain story are particularly important for working with scenarios (see Chapter 3, "Scenario-Based Modeling"). They will help you to set the scene: What is the story about? Why is it relevant? Which events trigger the story? Which constraints determine the plot of the story? What distinguishes this specific story from other possible stories?

If you look at the Metropolis 2 (see Figure 1.10) example again, you will recognize that app developer Anna and movie theater manager Matthew made the following assumptions about the story:

- A moviegoer buys a ticket at the box office.
- The moviegoer does not have a subscription.
- The story is about the "happy path," meaning the cashier suggests acceptable seats and the moviegoer buys and receives their ticket.

Also, sentence 4 in Metropolis 2 (see Figure 1.10) ("Cashier suggests available seats to moviegoer") has been annotated with "and mentions language." This is an example of an annotation that concerns a specific activity.

Annotations about the domain story as a whole are usually put on the margins or below the story. Annotations about a detail of the story are usually put right next to that particular element. When this gets too messy (which often happens in an analog setting), these detailed annotations are also put beside or below the story, using the according sequence number for reference. The next section shows an example for annotations on the margins (see Figure 2.8).

Modeling Canvas

To draw a domain story, you will need some kind of **modeling canvas** (see Figure 2.7 and Figure 2.8) to draw it onto. It doesn't have to be an actual canvas but can be a piece of paper, a whiteboard, etc. Also, it could be analog or digital. (We will go deeper into that in Chapter 5, "Modeling Tools.")

A typical first step is to give the domain story a **name** and to put it on the canvas.[2] This will set the frame for the story told. The name may be revised and refined as the story evolves.

---

2. As you have seen in the domain stories Metropolis 1 (see Figure 1.9) and 2 (see Figure 1.10), in this book we write the name below the story as a caption to the respective figure. In a modeling workshop, it is more common to write it at the top of the story.

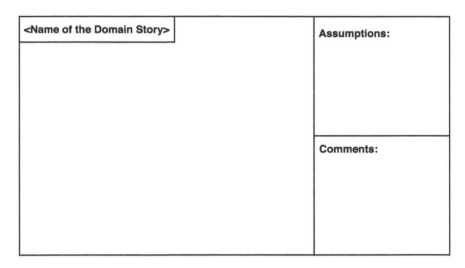

Figure 2.7 *Typical layout of the modeling canvas*

A good initial name expresses what's happening, using words from the domain language. Parts that may be added later are the company, a number, the case, the scope. (More on that in later chapters.)

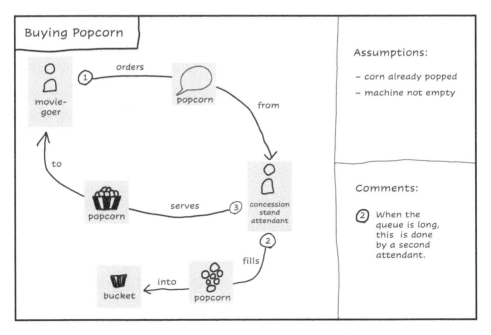

Figure 2.8 *Example of a modeling canvas layout on a whiteboard*

Groups

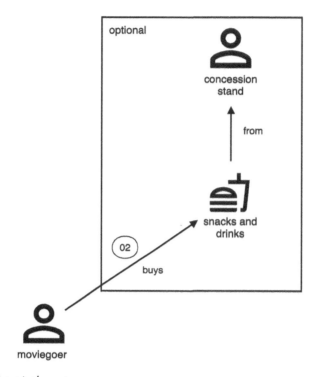

Figure 2.9 *A typical group*

A **group** (see Figure 2.9) is represented as an outline that clusters parts of a story that somehow belong together. The group can take any form, for example a rectangle, a circle, or a free-form shape. To describe the meaning of a group, label it accordingly. Here are some examples of what can be expressed by groups:

- Activities that are repeated
- Activities that are optional
- Parts of the story taking place in different locations
- Organizational boundaries
- Subdomains

For an example with groups, see Figure 2.10. It shows an enriched version of the high-level overview of the moviegoer's cinema experience. It now contains four groups that are used here to represent the different subdomains of the cinema domain. As this is a further development of Metropolis 1 (see Figure 1.9), we refer to this domain story as "Metropolis 1a" in the rest of the book.

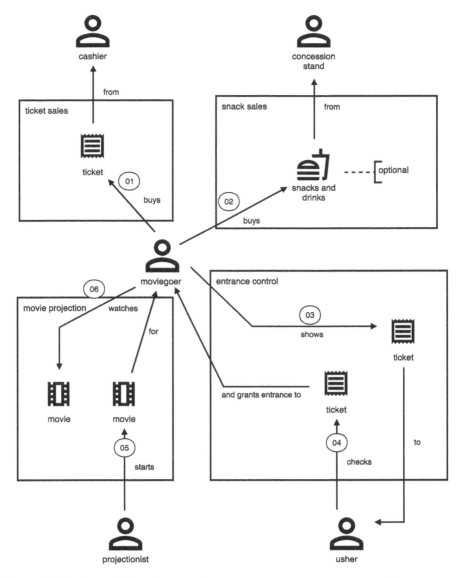

Figure 2.10 *Metropolis 1a: Going to the movies—*COARSE-GRAINED—*grouped by subdomain*

Colors

Figure 2.11 *Typical use of color*

Many domain stories are black and white only. Sometimes it makes sense to add a little more **color** (see Figure 2.11). Color can be used in the following ways:

- To emphasize some elements
- To visualize differences
- As an alternative to groups

You saw the use of gray and black as colors in Chapter 1 when we developed Metropolis 1 step-by-step (see Figures 1.1–1.9). There we used it to emphasize what has changed between two domain stories.

Now, app developer Anna wants to know from movie theater manager Matthew how legal requirements apply to the cinema. They use visual highlighting[3] to indicate which parts of a domain story have to follow which regulations. The result is Metropolis 1b (see Figure 2.12), which shows the requirements to food safety and fire protection.

Later in this book, we will use colors to visualize differences between versions of the same business process (see Chapter 13, "Supporting Organizational Change," and Chapter 14, "Deciding Make or Buy and Choosing Off-the-Shelf Software").

The choice of modeling tool determines what colors are available. In a black-and-white situation (like in a printed book), using grayscale may be the right choice.

When using different colors in a domain story, it can help to add a **legend** noting the meaning of each color. Figure 2.12 shows an example of a legend on the left.

---

3. For production reasons, while the e-book edition of this book contains colors, the print edition uses grayscale instead.

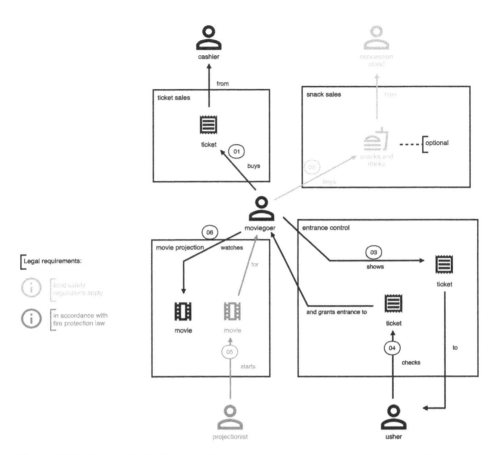

Figure 2.12 *Metropolis 1b: Going to the movies—*COARSE-GRAINED—*color shows legal requirements*

No Conditionals

Besides showing the elements of the pictographic language, we also want to point out what is *not* part of the pictographic language. There are no symbols for conditionals, variations, or alternatives. They are intentionally left out. This is a big difference compared to many other modeling approaches for business processes. For example, Business Process Model and Notation (BPMN) has *gateways* (see Figure 2.13).

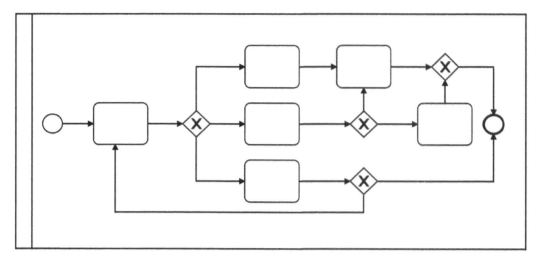

Figure 2.13 *The classical (**Not**-Domain-Storytelling) approach: modeling different cases in one diagram. (Here: A control flow with four gateways, modeled in BPMN.)*

We have observed that if a notation offers conditionals to model alternatives, people most likely will use them.[4] With Domain Storytelling, you model just the most important alternatives—each one as an individual domain story, told from beginning to end. We will elaborate on that in Chapter 3, "Scenario-Based Modeling."

Putting It All Together

 Domain stories visualize *who* (actor) does *what* (activity) with *what* (work objects) with *whom* (other actors).

The actors are the subjects of the sentences. In a Domain Storytelling workshop, representatives of the actors will be present, and they will identify with the stick

---

4. To be fair, BPMN and similar methods do not force you to use gateways. In fact, some authors consider it a best practice that the first version of a model should focus on one case only. See, for example, *Real-Life BPMN* [Freund/Rücker 2019].

figures in the domain story. Hence, the actors should be easy to spot. We recommend drawing them larger than the work objects.

> Domain stories evolve around the actors.

Every actor appears only once in the domain story. But for every activity, we draw a separate work object (even if the same work object already exists in a previous sentence). For example, look again at domain story Metropolis 1a (see Figure 2.10). The moviegoer appears only once, although that actor initiates several activities. The ticket, on the other hand, appears several times: It is bought, shown to the usher, and checked.

> Actors appear once per domain story; work objects can appear several times.

If you follow that rule, arranging work objects and arrows becomes a lot easier. There is another good reason for this. As the story evolves, a work object may change its status or representation. To illustrate that, let's look at a cutout of Metropolis 2 (see Figure 1.10) in Figure 2.14.

Here, the "available seats" are modeled as a seat icon in sentence 3, when the cashier searches for them. In sentence 4, where the cashier suggests seats to the moviegoer, they are modeled as a speech bubble.

A Grammar for Domain Stories

Activities connect actors and work objects to form **sentences**. Every sentence starts with an actor who initiates an activity: *who* (actor) does *what* (activity) with *what* (work objects) with *whom* (other actors). The basic syntax is: *subject – predicate – object*.[5] More complex syntax is allowed as well. Figure 2.15 shows a list of grammatically correct sentences for a domain story.

---

5. The syntax fits well within English grammar. Of course, there are languages that use differently structured sentences (e.g., *subject – object – predicate* in Farsi). If you tell a domain story in such a language, there will be a difference between the spoken language and its depiction in the pictographic language. See Chapter 9, "Learning Domain Language," for examples.

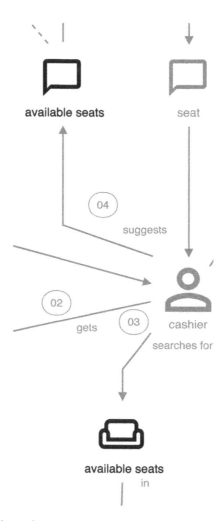

Figure 2.14 *A work object changes its representation*

The sentences in Figure 2.15 can be read as follows:

1. Actor *A* works on work object *w* (creates it, buys it, processes it, looks something up in it…).

2. Actor *A* works on work object *w* to edit work object *v*.

3. Actor *A* hands work object *w* over to actor *B*, or *A* exchanges information about *w* with *B*. Often, a preposition (e.g., *to*, *with*, *in*) is a fitting label for the second arrow.

4. This is the same as sentence 3 but with several recipients.

5. The two actors *A* and *B* collaborate on *w* (sign it, agree on it…).

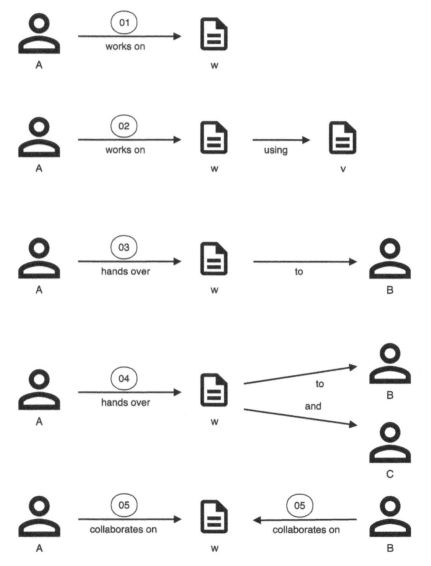

Figure 2.15 *Possible sentence structures*

Different Styles of Drawing

In sentences 2 to 5 in Figure 2.15, we use two arrows even though the actor performs only one activity. This little discrepancy is due to the use of a modeling tool. If you record your domain story by hand, you can draw one arrow from actor to actor and then place the work object on top of the arrow (see Figure 2.16).

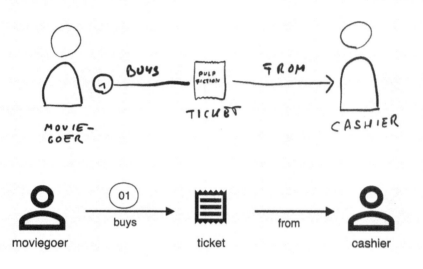

Figure 2.16 *Different style, same meaning: hand-drawn vs. tool-drawn*

Another difference that you might spot is the placement of the sequence number. In the hand-drawn version, it is positioned at the beginning of the activity's arrow. In the tool-drawn version, it is placed on top of the activity's label.

The grammar should help with translating domain knowledge into pictographic language. But the expressiveness of a domain story is more important than the correctness of the grammar.

 Keep in mind that each sentence should make sense if you read it out loud.

We consider it good practice to speak during modeling—"modeling out loud," as the inventor of Domain-Driven Design, Eric Evans, calls it:

> The detachment of speech from other forms of communication is a particularly great loss because we humans have a genius for spoken language. [...] One of the best ways to refine a model is to explore with speech, trying out loud various constructs from possible model variations. Rough edges are easy to hear. [Evans 2004]

To summarize, domain stories should be modeled on the spoken language (with the limitations given earlier concerning grammatical differences between natural languages and the pictographic language).

Good Language Style

In our experience, the pictographic language is more about expressiveness than about adherence to strict rules. However, we think it is useful to show you examples of what we consider good style and what we consider poor style. We have added reasons why you should consider our suggestions—at least until you have enough experience to make your own conscious choices.

Give Every Sentence Its Own Work Objects

If you look again at the domain stories Metropolis 1 (see Figure 1.9) and 2 (see Figure 1.10), you will see that work objects like "ticket" and "seating plan" appear several times. Every activity that relates to a ticket has its own work object, depicting a ticket (rather than there being just one "ticket" work object for the whole domain story). There are good reasons for that:

- First, you might want to represent a work object with different icons (e.g., the ticket could be issued in the form of a QR code and printed later).
- Second, having several arrows going in and out of work objects reduces the readability of the story.
- Third, when every sentence has its own work objects, they can be clustered into groups without overlapping.

Hence, we favor giving every sentence its own work objects over reusing work objects.

Make Work Objects Explicit

We have said that activities represent the verbs in the pictographic language and that work objects are, well, the objects. Sentences can have more than one object in natural languages, and that is also true for the pictographic language (see, for example, the second sentence in Figure 2.15).

However, we noticed that Domain Storytelling novices tend to stick to the basic sentence structure of *actor – activity – work object*. If there is a second object involved, they often make it an implicit part of the activity. Take a look at the example in Figure 2.17.

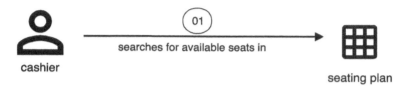

Figure 2.17 *Don't: model work object as part of activity*

The activity "searches for available seats in" contains the word "seats." For a cinema, "seat" is an important piece of the domain language: Seats are searched for, reserved, sold, and so on. Hence, it makes sense to make this explicit by modeling it as a work object, as shown in Figure 2.18.

Figure 2.18 *Do: model work object separate from activity*

Sometimes, work objects do not hide in activities but in other work objects, like in Figure 2.19. That too is something you should avoid.

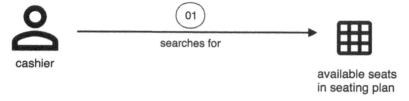

Figure 2.19 *Don't: model work object as part of another work object*

In Part II of this book, you will learn to use Domain Storytelling for specific purposes, such as finding boundaries within a domain or deriving an implementable model from domain stories. These practices rely on a proper mapping of domain concepts to the pictographic language.

Provide a Label for Every Building Block

We have recommended that you label all actors, activities, work objects, and groups with terms from the domain language. It is tempting to omit some obvious or unimportant terms to speed up modeling. But beware, what is obvious to you is not necessarily obvious to other people. It is easier to spot different interpretations of terms if you put them in writing. Also, what seems obvious now may be confusing in a week or a month. If you revisit your domain stories later, you will be thankful if the whole story is spelled out and not just implied. Therefore, we prefer readability over brevity.

Use Different Icons for Actors and Work Objects

Even though a concise pictographic language has its advantages (i.e., fewer icons and meanings to memorize), you should not go as far as to use the same icon for actors *and* work objects. This would be confusing and affect readability.

Avoid "Loopbacks"

When it comes to modeling a software system's activities, modelers with a programming background will sometimes apply the pattern shown in Figure 2.20.

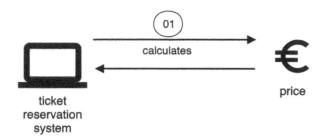

Figure 2.20 *Don't: model function call*

However, the arrows in the pictographic language do not represent a function, method, or procedure call. Hence, there is no need for this "loopback" pattern. A system that calculates a price can simply be modeled like in Figure 2.21.

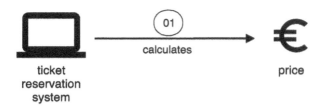

Figure 2.21 *Do: model activity*

Avoid the "Request and Response" Pattern

Software developers seem to have a tendency to model the interaction between a software system and a user as something technical—a request that is fulfilled by the system's response. For example, a web app for buying movie tickets modeled in that style would look something like Figure 2.22.

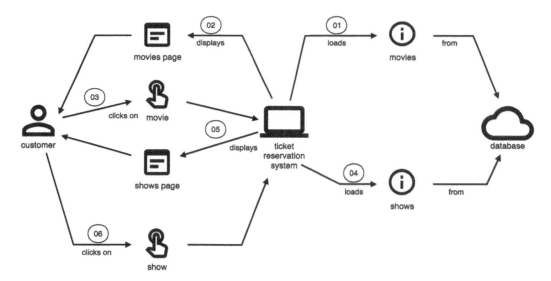

Figure 2.22 *Don't: model the technical details of how a user interacts with a system*

There are several reasons why we do not like this style so much:

- It does not tell a compelling story. It has little potential to spark interesting conversations and insights about the domain.
- If the goal of the model is to document the implementation of the system, then there are better ways of achieving this, e.g., a Unified Modeling Language (UML) sequence diagram.

- If the goal of the model is to design the user interface, then there are better means to do that (e.g., mock-ups and prototypes).

- Since the model is specific to the technical implementation of the software system, it will be outdated if the implementation changes.

Instead, use Domain Storytelling to model intent: What is the goal of the user? How does the software system help them to reach that goal? Each activity should push the story forward. (See Figure 2.23.)

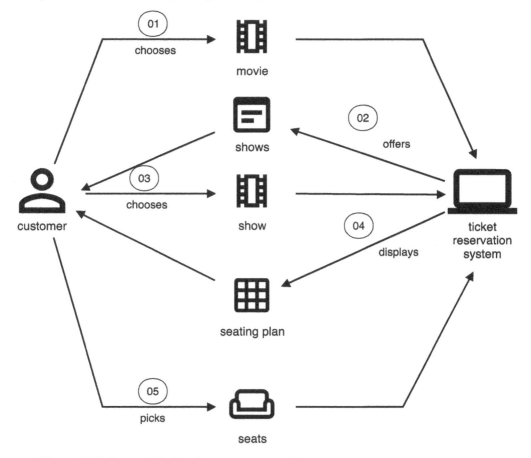

Figure 2.23 *Do: model what the user wants to achieve*

Now that you know the building blocks of the pictographic language, let's move on to the special Domain Storytelling way of modeling different cases.

Chapter 3

Scenario-Based Modeling

As we explained in the previous chapter, the pictographic language gets by without symbols for conditionals, variations, or alternatives. With Domain Storytelling, you model just the most important alternatives—each one as an individual domain story. As Cyrille Martraire put it in *Living Documentation*, "One diagram, one story" [Martraire 2019]. If you are used to *flowcharts*, *BPMN*, or *UML activity diagrams*, a diagram that shows just one possible path might seems awkward at first. However, a *UML sequence diagram* does exactly it—shows a single path of execution. Actually, scenario-based modeling has a long tradition in software development. *Use cases*, for example, are also scenario-based.

What Are Scenarios?

John Carroll describes **scenarios** as follows [Carroll 2000]:

- Scenarios are stories about people and their activities.
- Scenarios take place in a fixed context.
- Scenarios contain actors that typically have goals.
- Scenarios have a plot. They consist of a sequence of activities and events.

Domain stories are scenarios in that sense. We use the terms *story* and *scenario* interchangeably in this book. They are concrete, meaningful examples of a business process (see Figure 3.1).

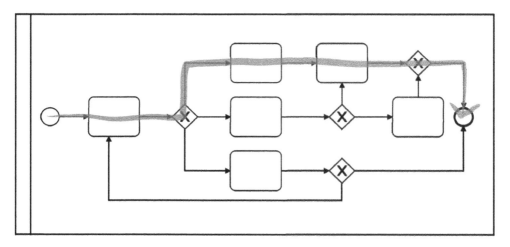

Figure 3.1 *A scenario is one instance of a business process*

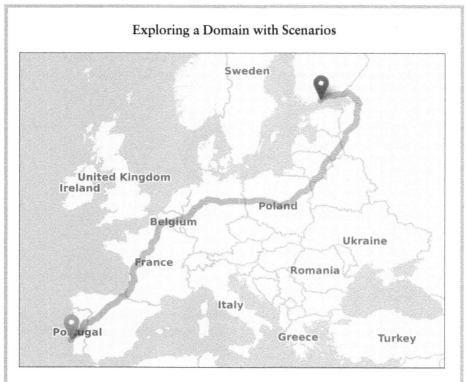

Figure 3.2 *A journey through Europe as an example of a scenario. Picture taken from OpenStreetMap.org*

Think about traveling through Europe[1] as an analogy: Europe is the domain that you want to explore. If you take the route we have marked on the map in Figure 3.2, from Lisbon to Helsinki, you will cover a lot of countries and landscapes (the subdomains) and cross many borders. Still, you will completely miss many countries, the entire Alps, the Mediterranean Sea, and much more. To get a sound understanding of Europe's boundaries, you will need to make several comprehensive journeys—or, in other words, model several scenarios.

Scenarios in Domain Storytelling

When we model a business process, every possible instance of that process could be described in the form of a scenario or domain story. But what do we do if several important alternatives need to be covered? How do we narrow down the vast number of instances? We will take another look at the cinema example to illustrate our approach.

The movie theater Metropolis sells (a) tickets for single shows and (b) yearly subscriptions. This means app developer Anna cannot simply ask movie theater manager Matthew to tell her a story about a moviegoer who approaches the cashier. Instead, she asks him which case is more common, and he tells her that selling tickets for single shows makes up 75% of his revenue. Therefore, Anna asks Matthew to tell her about this case and writes down "ticket sales" on the whiteboard—the name for the domain story.

While she is recording the story, additional assumptions are made to avoid drifting off to different story lines. For example, they assume that enough seats are available, that the moviegoer likes the seats the cashier offers, and so on: "Assuming that there are still seats available, what do you do next?" Anna writes all these assumptions down as annotations.

We recommend you start with modeling the default case—the "80% case"—and the "happy path" first.

That should give you a general idea of the purpose of the process. It will help you to understand *why* the actors are doing all this. Narrow the case down—no

---

1. We thank Jörn Koch for this analogy.

exceptions, no errors, the sun is shining, everything is fine. Later, you can ask what could go wrong, and you can model important variations and error cases as separate domain stories. For example, if shows in a cinema are sometimes overbooked, you definitely want to look into that case.

Usually, a few domain stories are sufficient to understand a business process. One or a handful of COARSE-GRAINED domain stories will help you to figure out where to dig deeper and what other resources you will need. Often, you only need to add a few FINE-GRAINED stories to start prototyping.

Small variations in a business process such as optional activities are simply not worth the effort of modeling them separately. Instead, you should use annotations.

At the Metropolis, Anna and Matthew model the variation of the previous assumption—the case "there are no more seats available"—as a domain story in its own right. This results in Metropolis 3 (see Figure 3.3).

If it helps participants to commit to one story line, you can make assumptions about the story as a whole *and* annotate the sentence where an assumption comes into play. For example, Metropolis 3 is about a case where there are no seats available (an assumption about the story as a whole). Additionally, the third sentence ("The cashier searches for available seats in the seating plan.") is annotated with "Assumption: No seats available."

As you can see, it started as a copy of the happy path Metropolis 2 (see Figure 1.10). The first three sentences are the same. In step 3, Anna adds an annotation that no seats are available. From there on, the story line differs. To make that visible, let's place Metropolis 2 (see Figure 1.10) and 3 (see Figure 3.3) side by side in Figure 3.4.

If large parts of two stories overlap, it may be better not to duplicate all the steps in the new story. Starting the story from the first step that differs is also a possibility. This is especially true if you are working with an analog modeling tool that makes copying a cumbersome task.

Of course, there is also value in "algorithmic" descriptions of business processes, and one cannot develop software without thinking about conditionals. But premature abstractions are often wrong and not useful for understanding a domain. Bad abstractions obscure the domain; good abstractions add precision to the domain language.

First establish a sound understanding of *typical* cases—tell stories. Only then discuss *what else* could happen—collect rules.

A method that may help with finding such rules is *Example Mapping* (see Chapter 7, "Relationship to Other Modeling Methods," for more details).

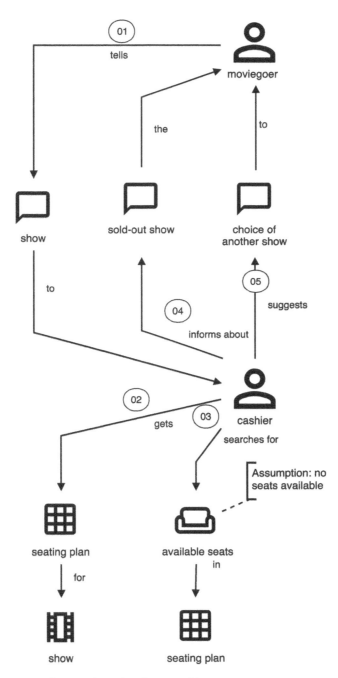

Figure 3.3 *Metropolis 3: Ticket sales, show is sold out—*FINE-GRAINED

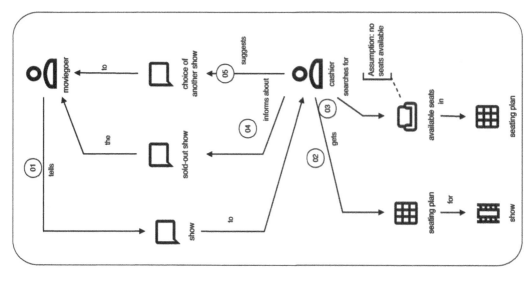

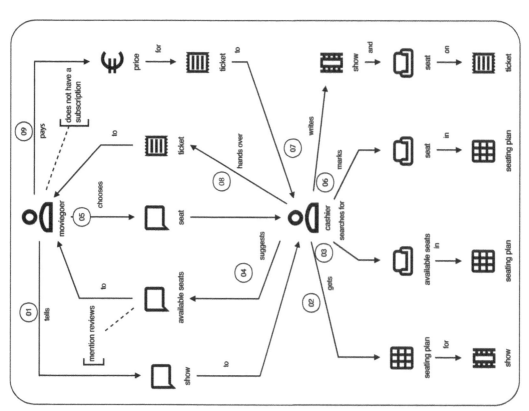

Figure 3.4 *The Domain Storytelling approach: modeling different cases in different stories: Metropolis 2 and 3*

Concrete Examples as Scenarios

In some domains, it can be difficult to identify scenarios like "typical case" and "happy path." In such situations, we recommend a different approach. Try to model several past cases with increasing complexity: a simple case, a moderately difficult case, and a difficult case.

Once, when we were developing software for an emergency task force at a port, we naïvely asked the domain experts for common cases and happy paths. They shrugged and said, "We deal exclusively with the unexpected and with exceptions to the rules." So we asked them to give us three examples for emergencies they'd had to deal with in the last year, from simple to complex:

- A loose container drifting in the harbor
- A blackout that affects the rail system during a heavy storm; a train is stuck in an area that is at risk of being flooded
- A freighter stranded and in danger of bursting, potentially polluting the harbor

For every scenario, they told us a rich domain story with increasing complexity.

Keeping an Overview

To avoid modeling an overwhelming number of scenarios, it is important to restrict yourself to modeling only the most important variations of a business process.

Aim for a representative sample, not for completeness!

When you need to model several complex businesses and each has several important variations, you will end up with dozens of domain stories. It is useful to organize them in a way that helps you keep an overview. Here are some strategies that have worked for us:

- As you have already seen, a COARSE-GRAINED domain story like Metropolis 1 (see Figure 1.9) can serve as an anchor for more detailed domain stories (like Metropolis 2, shown in Figure 1.10, and Metropolis 3, shown in Figure 3.3).
- Many companies use wikis to organize and document knowledge. A wiki makes it easy to build hierarchical structures and navigate within them using

hyperlinks. Domain stories can also be organized with a wiki. Take photographs from drawn diagrams or use the files created directly with a digital tool.

- If many different actors are involved, it can be useful to check at a glance who is involved in which scenarios. UML's *use case diagrams* can provide such an overview [Rumbaugh et al. 2005]. In a use case diagram, you can put together all the actors who play a role in your domain stories. Figure 3.5 shows an example for the Metropolis cinema.[3] It contains two use cases, represented as ellipses—"ticket sales" and "subscription sales." Both use cases involve a cashier and a moviegoer, represented as stick figures. The "ticket sales" use case was covered with two scenarios ("happy path" and "show is sold out"). Hence, the ellipsis contains not only the name of the use case, but also the name of the domain stories in which the scenarios were modeled (Metropolis 2 and 3). That way, the two types of diagrams are linked, and the use case diagram provides an overview that tells you which actors are involved in which domain stories.

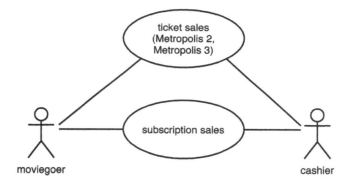

Figure 3.5 *Use case diagram for Metropolis*

Now you know how to get an overview of FINE-GRAINED domain stories. Let's look more closely at that granularity and other properties of domain stories.

---

2. We would not necessarily model a use case diagram in real life if there were just a handful of domain stories and two actors.

Chapter 4

Scope

Domain Storytelling is not a "one-size-fits-all" approach. In this chapter, we will discuss the level of detail that stories have, whether they are descriptive or exploratory, and the amount of technical information they contain. We will call all of these factors the **scope** of a domain story. The scope or parts of the scope are often reflected in the name of a domain story. Let's look at the factors that determine the scope.

Granularity

So far, you have seen several domain stories from the cinema domain. Metropolis 1 models a high-level view, where buying a ticket is just one activity. (Here we look at its variant with subdomains, Metropolis 1a; see Figure 2.10.) Metropolis 2 (see Figure 1.10) elaborates that activity into a whole domain story: It shows in detail how a moviegoer buys a ticket at the box office. Figure 4.1 visualizes this refinement.

As you can see, the level of detail varies from story to story. This level of detail is expressed in the scope factor **granularity**. Domain stories can be COARSE-GRAINED, FINE-GRAINED, and everything in between, e.g., MEDIUM-GRAINED. The spectrum is continuous. But if you find yourself modeling detailed interactions between users and systems (e.g., "customer clicks button") or interactions between objects (as in a UML sequence diagram), then you have probably gone too far.

Always aim for a consistent level of detail throughout a story. Mixing FINE-GRAINED and COARSE-GRAINED activities can be confusing and indicative of a larger problem—e.g., the COARSE-GRAINED parts may indicate that some knowledge holders were not present at the workshop. If this is the case, annotate the story and fill in the gap in another session with people who have the necessary knowledge.

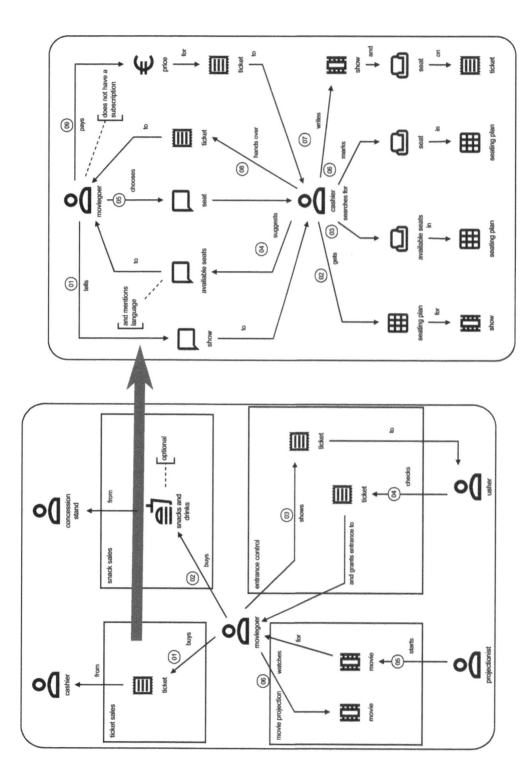

Figure 4.1 *From Metropolis 1a to Metropolis 2: An activity from a COARSE-GRAINED story is detailed in a FINE-GRAINED story*

A Useful Metaphor for Granularity

Distinguishing different levels of granularity with terms like FINE-GRAINED and COARSE-GRAINED has limited expressiveness. In *Writing Effective Use Cases*, Alistair Cockburn introduces a metaphor for granularity that can also help with domain stories [Cockburn 2001]. Cockburn defines so-called *goal levels* by using the ocean as a metaphor (see Figure 4.2). You start at *sea level*. A sea-level goal describes something a user wants to achieve. When you get more COARSE-GRAINED, you ascend to *kite* and *cloud level*, which are summaries of sea-level goals. Going more FINE-GRAINED, you descend below sea level to *fish level*. Finally, at the bottom of the ocean lies the *clam level* (which Cockburn also calls "too low").

Figure 4.2 *Different goal levels*[1]

These metaphors are of course not meant as an exact measure for granularity. But, to give you some idea:

- For Cockburn, a sea-level use case is something that can be achieved by the user in one go. A kite-level use case takes the user more than one sitting with the software.

- For us, the Metropolis 1 example hovers at kite level, and the Metropolis 2 example floats at sea level (see Figure 4.1).

- At cloud level, you might model the whole organization Metropolis as a single actor (not differentiating between departments, roles, and software systems).

---

1. The icons are taken from Wikipedia [Wikipedia Cockburn-Style] and were created by Menner under Creative Commons CC0.

As a moderator, you can bring these metaphors into play whenever the scope seems unclear. Draw the icons from Figure 4.2 on sticky notes and post them on a wall in the meeting room. The icons serve as a constant reminder: "At what level of detail do we need to discuss this?" Once these metaphors are established, you may hear people saying things like, "Let's bring this kite down to sea level!" or "This is not the time to dive to fish level!" It can make sense to add the goal-level metaphor to a domain story, either as an icon or as part of a story's name.[2]

Since COARSE-GRAINED stories cover a lot of ground, storytellers from different departments or even different organizations should participate in a workshop. Up to 15 storytellers is common in such cases. The number of storytellers in a workshop for FINE-GRAINED stories is usually smaller, i.e., around two to seven people. Often the storytellers are from only one (or a few) business departments. But even if we focus just on one department, there might be different roles that need to be represented.

Point in Time (As-Is vs. To-Be)

Both Metropolis 1 and Metropolis 2 (see Figure 4.1) describe a process as it currently is. Domain stories can also describe how it will (possibly) look in the future. This **point in time** is another scope factor of a domain story (see Figure 4.3).

Figure 4.3 *Scope factor point in time*

The current situation is often called the *problem space* because the intent of modeling is to improve something that is bad or to solve a problem. Domain stories that model the problem space are called AS-IS stories. Possible improved situations can also be explored with the help of domain stories. Hence, such TO-BE processes describe the *solution space*.

---

2. In modern Unicode there are even emoji for it. Probably it's good advice to be careful and not use them in filenames, though.

We chose the word pairs AS-IS/TO-BE and *problem/solution space* because they are established in the business process modeling community and in the Domain-Driven Design community (see, for example, *Implementing Domain-Driven Design* [Vernon 2013]). You may have come across other word pairs that have the same intention: *descriptive* versus *exploratory* or *informational* versus *aspirational*.

Usually, AS-IS means the situation at the time of modeling—at a certain point in time. TO-BE, on the other hand, is a look ahead. There can be different points in the future that may be interesting to model as separate TO-BE domain stories (see Figure 4.4). Also, you may look at alternative models that explore the same point in time. This is useful for comparing different possible solutions and finding the best one.

Often, the different points in time are chosen because something will be accomplished or changed by then; e.g., a new software system will be operational. The point in time is sometimes added to the name of a domain story.

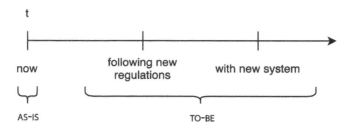

Figure 4.4 *Example points in time of a domain story*

Workshops in which TO-BE stories are told should involve the future actors—e.g., the (future) users of the software system that is being developed. Other stakeholders such as product owners are also valuable.

Domain Purity (PURE vs. DIGITALIZED)

Looking back at the Metropolis example again, we saw that app developer Anna and movie theater manager Matthew modeled two AS-IS stories in the first workshop: the COARSE-GRAINED (or kite-level) Metropolis 1 and the FINE-GRAINED (or sea-level) Metropolis 2 (see Figure 4.1). Did you realize that Anna did not model any software systems that Matthew has used? Surely even a small cinema like the Metropolis must run some kind of IT, even if it is just a spreadsheet. But Anna did not forget to ask Matthew about the software he uses. In fact, Anna made a deliberate choice. When modeling domain stories, you either include or omit (existing or yet to be built) software. This scope factor is called **domain purity**. We call domain stories without software systems PURE, and those with software systems DIGITALIZED.

PURE domain stories are particularly helpful for building new software systems. They allow you to understand a domain without also internalizing the accidental complexity added by existing software. To lift the veil of software off the domain, the experts should talk about how things *would* be done if all activities were motivated only by the domain (and not by the existing software systems).

For domains that existed before software was ubiquitous, do a thought experiment: Ask for stories that tell how things were done in the pen-and-paper days. Focus on provoking thoughts, not on historical accuracy.

In DIGITALIZED domain stories, the actors can be people or software systems. That means software functionality and its shortcomings are part of the story. In Figure 4.5, for example, the IT system "cinema website" is modeled as an actor.

In many organizations, the domain model is buried under decades of badly modeled software systems. You can use DIGITALIZED AS-IS domain stories to visualize and talk about this mess. Find out which activities are not motivated by the domain but required in order to work with the present software systems. Identify language that was introduced by software developers and is not rooted in the domain. That is where annotations come into play because they help to explain *why* people are doing what they are doing.

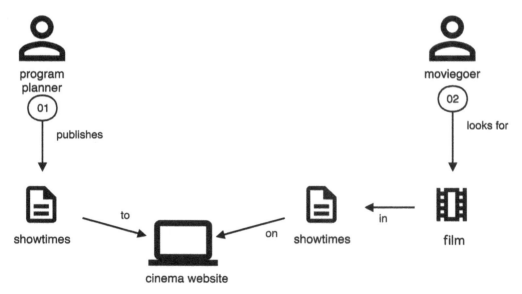

Figure 4.5 *Domain stories with software systems as actors are called* DIGITALIZED

When you want to explore or show how a new software system would change the work, DIGITALIZED TO-BE domain stories will help you. They are often a further development of a PURE AS-IS story—one to which the system is added.

Combining the Scope Factors: A Typical Journey

The factors that determine the scope can be combined in many ways. Mathematically speaking, the scope is a cross product:

$$Scope = Granularity \times DomainPurity \times PointInTime$$

We are going to describe typical scopes of domain stories and how you can travel from one scope to the next:

- COARSE-GRAINED, PURE, AS-IS
- FINE-GRAINED, PURE, AS-IS
- FINE-GRAINED, DIGITALIZED, TO-BE

These are only examples of different types of domain stories, with no strict definitions. Hence, this is not the only possible journey. Feel free to adapt. Also, you do not have to use Domain Storytelling in a sequence from COARSE-GRAINED TO FINE-GRAINED. Modeling is usually an iterative process, and you may change the scope as needed. We will show you another example of a journey through different scopes in Part II: "Using and Adapting Domain Storytelling for Different Purposes."

Explore a New Domain (COARSE-GRAINED, PURE, AS-IS)

The first Domain Storytelling workshop in a company, a department, or a development project often takes a COARSE-GRAINED view at the problem space. Stories like that help to get your bearings. Usually, it is helpful to omit software systems to see the naked domain itself.

Since organizations serve a purpose, it is a good idea to look at the primary purpose from the viewpoint of the organization's customers. Hence, COARSE-GRAINED domain stories often illustrate an end-to-end business process. That is why Metropolis 1 (see Figure 1.9) tells a story from buying a ticket for a movie to watching it. If you are uncertain what "end-to-end" really means, you can get the conversation going by explicitly adding a few extra sentences at the beginning and at the end.

COARSE-GRAINED, PURE, AS-IS stories can serve several purposes:

- They are a starting point for exploring the domain (*knowledge crunching*).

- They provide an overview of several FINE-GRAINED domain stories (see Chapter 3, "Scenario-Based Modeling").

- They can be analyzed to find boundaries (see Chapter 10) in the domain. You saw a brief example of that in Metropolis 1a (see Figure 2.10), which shows subdomains of the cinema domain. Subdomains can be used as boundaries in teams and boundaries in software—for example, designing a new system in a modular way, splitting a *big ball of mud* [Foote/Yoder 1997] into modules, or splitting a monolith into microservices.

Drill Down into Subdomains (FINE-GRAINED, PURE, AS-IS)

After you've roughly found your way around a domain and established a common understanding of a project's extent, you can drill into the details. Instead of looking at the domain as a whole, you should focus on a selected subdomain. For example, Anna and Matthew drilled down into the ticket sales subdomain when they modeled Metropolis 2 (see Figure 1.10) and Metropolis 3 (see Figure 3.3).

Many companies are organized by subdomains, which means FINE-GRAINED AS-IS stories often take place within one department. However, it can be interesting to add an extra sentence at the beginning and at the end of the story. By doing so, you can take a look at the interface between subdomains or departments. This will help you to understand how people work together across department boundaries.

FINE-GRAINED, PURE, AS-IS stories show *how* people work together *today* (i.e., in the problem space). Such stories are useful in several ways:

- You can find out which business processes could benefit from improved software support. This is often a starting point for conversations about software requirements (see Chapter 11).

- You can distill a technologically untainted domain model from them and implement the model in code (see Chapter 12).

- By comparing AS-IS with TO-BE domain stories, you can visualize how work will change (see the next section).

Introduce New Software (FINE-GRAINED, DIGITALIZED, TO-BE)

A common way of using domain stories is to tell how things should change. Stories can be about improved processes, new roles, or new software.

The Metropolis, for example, wants to introduce an app for moviegoers. Obviously, Anna and Matthew will want to model how moviegoers would use the app as a FINE-GRAINED, DIGITALIZED, TO-BE domain story. However, the app will also impact the box office. After all, tickets for the same shows will be sold via two sales channels—the moviegoer app and the box office. This will go well only if the cashiers use a box-office app that works together with the moviegoer app. Hence, Anna and Matthew revisit the box-office sales process they modeled as a PURE AS-IS domain story—Metropolis 2 (see Figure 1.10). From it, they derive a DIGITALIZED TO-BE version of the box-office sales process—Metropolis 4 (see Figure 4.6).

As you can see, sentences 2, 3, and 6 must be supported by the box-office app. These are the first requirements for that app.

FINE-GRAINED, DIGITALIZED, TO-BE stories show how people and software systems should work together *in the future*. This is useful for a variety of purposes:

- Visualizing how the work will change once the improvements are implemented. FINE-GRAINED, DIGITALIZED, TO-BE stories often complement FINE-GRAINED, PURE AS-IS stories—they are at the same level of detail (about sea level), but with systems and in the solution space. (Read on in Chapter 13, "Supporting Organizational Change.")
- Working with requirements (see Chapter 11).
- Modeling the domain in code (see Chapter 12).
- Deciding make or buy and choosing off-the-shelf software (see Chapter 14).

Summarizing the Journey

You have now read about three different scopes, each illustrated by a domain story about Metropolis. Table 4.1 shows an overview of the journey.

Table 4.1 *Overview of the Metropolis Domain Stories*

Goal	Domain stories	Granularity	Point in Time	Domain Purity
Explore a new domain	Metropolis 1 (see Figure 1.9) and 1a (see Figure 2.10)	COARSE-GRAINED	AS-IS	PURE
Drill down into subdomains	Metropolis 2 (see Figure 1.10) and 3 (see Figure 3.3)	FINE-GRAINED	AS-IS	PURE
Introduce new software	Metropolis 4 (see Figure 4.6)	FINE-GRAINED	TO-BE	DIGITALIZED

We hope that this chapter will guide you to find a scope that helps you with your modeling problem.

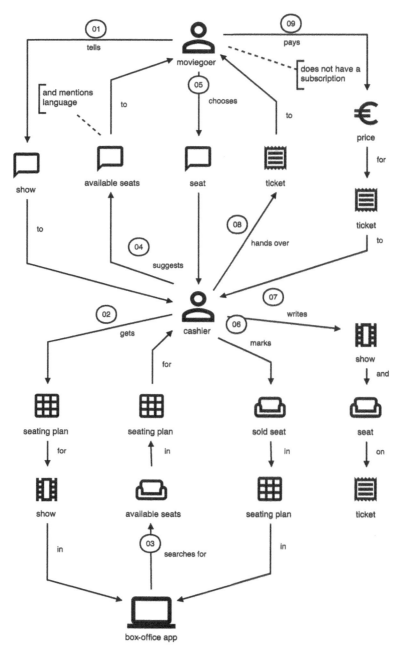

Figure 4.6 *Metropolis 4: Ticket sales, happy path*—FINE-GRAINED, DIGITALIZED, TO-BE

Chapter 5

Modeling Tools

So far, we have assumed that domain stories are documented on a modeling canvas, e.g., a whiteboard or with software. Over the years, we have tried many different **tools**. We will now take a closer look at the available options, their advantages, and their disadvantages. First, we discuss analog tools. Then, we introduce some software tools. The chapter ends with a few tips for choosing a tool.

Modeling on Paper or Boards

Paper, flip charts, boards, etc., are cheap and ubiquitous modeling tools (see Figure 5.1). They work well for spontaneous modeling sessions with a small group of people. As there are some limitations too, we would like to give you our recommendations for modeling with the following:

- Pen and paper
- Sticky notes on a flip chart or paper roll
- Just a whiteboard
- Sticky notes on whiteboard
- The "whiteboard kit"

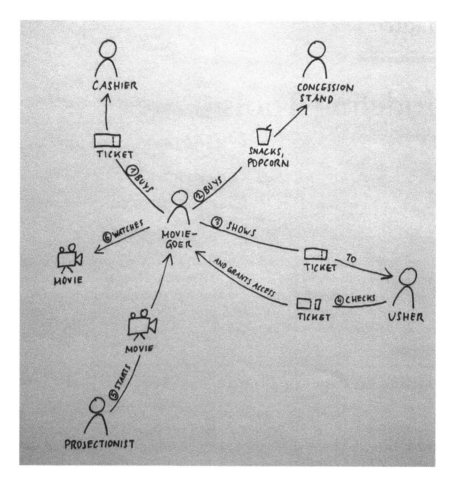

Figure 5.1 *Modeling on paper*

If you model alone and want to use Domain Storytelling as a thinking tool, pen and paper are all you need. Even if you model with one other person, a piece of paper will suffice. But as soon as there are three or more people involved, you will need a larger modeling canvas to enable everyone to see the domain story. This is when you want to switch to flip charts or a paper roll.

An obvious disadvantage of all paper-based modeling is that it is hard to revise the pictures. And you will need to revise them quite often, not only because domain experts correct their story as they go but also because even skilled modelers make mistakes. The moderator should also consider the layout of the picture in advance. For example, actors that are central to the story should be placed in the middle so that there is enough space to draw many incoming and outgoing arrows.

Using sticky notes for actors and work objects makes life a lot easier, especially if you use them on a whiteboard instead of paper (see Figure 5.2).

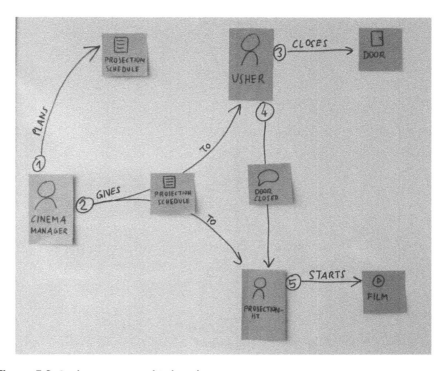

Figure 5.2 *Sticky notes on a whiteboard*

We've tried different ways of using sticky notes for Domain Storytelling on whiteboards. Here we highlight what has worked best for us.

We draw actors and work objects on sticky notes. Activities (arrows and labels) and sequence numbers go directly on the whiteboard. For us, this is the best compromise between ease of reorganizing and a clean and consistent look. We recommend you use square stickies for the work objects (see Figure 5.3) and larger, rectangular stickies for actors (see Figure 5.4). That makes the actors easily recognizable. Some practitioners favor using different colors to distinguish actors from work objects.

Another recommendation is to write a sentence's number at the beginning of an arrow, next to the actor who initiates the activity. Draw a circle around the number so it is easy to spot.

Whichever personal style you develop, key to understandable domain stories is to apply your style consistently.

Figure 5.3 *Put work objects on square sticky notes*

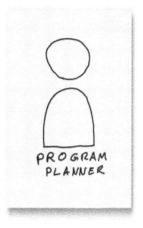

Figure 5.4 *Put actors on rectangular sticky notes*

Experimenting with Sticky Notes on Whiteboards

It took us a while to figure out what works and what doesn't. To spare you the hassle, we share our failures with you.

- **Sticky notes for everything:** We used large sticky notes for activities (arrows and labels) and smaller sticky notes for everything else. That did not work at all because it limits the layout of the domain stories too much.

- **Sticky notes for everything but the arrows:** We used sticky notes for actors, work objects, sequence numbers, and labels of activities, but the activity arrow was drawn directly on the whiteboard. That resulted in too much visual separation between an activity's arrow and the label.

- Sticky notes just for work objects: Since domain stories evolve around the actors, we thought there would be less need for changing the position of actors. We were wrong. Also, the story looks weird if some icons are on sticky notes (those for the work objects) and other icons are on the whiteboard (those for the actors).

- Sticky notes for actors, work objects, and sequence numbers: We used very small stickies for the numbers (instead of writing the numbers next to the arrows). The idea was to make the numbers even easier to spot. But we found that three kinds of sticky notes are difficult to handle and that the small stickies produce a lot of clutter.

Sticky notes make it easier to correct mistakes and change the layout, but you still need to draw the icons by hand. We noticed that many moderators tend to draw only a few icons and rely on the textual representation of actors and work objects. If it works for the given purpose, that may be fine, but we think that such pictures lack in richness of expression. Discussing how a work object is represented uncovers hidden assumptions. Drawing icons facilitates such discussions and is therefore valuable.

To overcome the disadvantage of drawing icons by hand, Stefan printed icons on paper and taped them onto the modeling canvas. A more sophisticated version of this became known as the **whiteboard kit** (see Figure 5.5). We printed icons on slightly thicker paper, laminated it, and glued little flat magnets to the back. These cards stick on a whiteboard, and if you write on them with a whiteboard marker, they are reusable. We published a template for our whiteboard kit on www.domainstorytelling.org [DomainStorytelling Website]. Of course, you can (and in fact *should*) adapt the icon set to fit your domain.

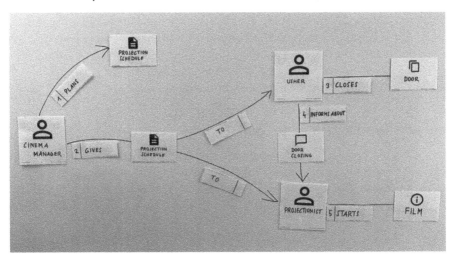

Figure 5.5 *Magnetic, laminated whiteboard kit*

Modeling on whiteboards or large paper has an advantage over digital tools: All participants have "write access" to the model. This means that analog tools enable shared and collaborative modeling—at least for a limited number of people (see Chapter 6, "The Workshop Format").

Modeling with Software Tools

Software tools fall into these categories:

- Digitalized hand-drawing (for example, with tablet and digital pen)
- General-purpose drawing tools
- Virtual, collaborative whiteboards
- Special-purpose modeling tools, like our very own *Egon.io—The Domain Story Modeler* [Egon.io Website]

Most software tools are designed for a single user who uses an input device (mouse, keyboard, pen, etc.). Since shared modeling is not possible with such tools, one person needs to play the role of the *modeler* (see Chapter 6, "The Workshop Format") and do the drawing. As with analog tools, the model should be visible for all participants. That means you need to connect the modeler's computer to a projector. Exceptions are virtual whiteboards and digital blackboards.

Digitalized Hand-Drawing

Digitalized hand-drawing (see Figure 5.6) can be done with a big touchscreen and a digital pen, like the Microsoft Surface Hub, or a tablet and digital pen, like the iPad and the Apple Pencil. It combines the freedom of drawing everything you want with the capability for easy change (i.e., moving parts of the domain story around without having to redraw it). Some people also like that they do not have to follow the rules and limitations that some modeling tools enforce.

General-Purpose Drawing Tools

There is a wide range of general-purpose drawing tools that can be used to record domain stories graphically. Some popular tools that fall into this category are Gliffy, yEd, diagrams.net, Microsoft Visio, and even Microsoft PowerPoint (see Figure 5.7).

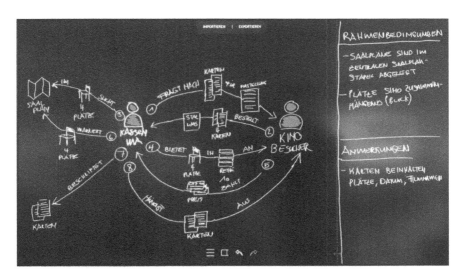

Figure 5.6 *Domain Storytelling with a digital blackboard*

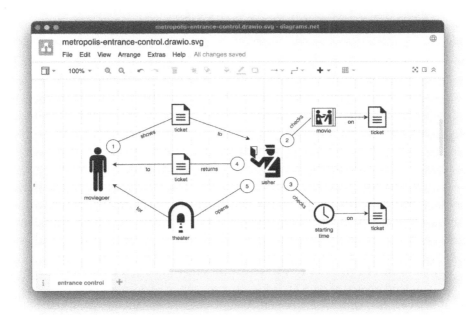

Figure 5.7 *Modeling with diagrams.net*

In our experience, there is no general-purpose tool that stands out when it comes to modeling domain stories. Hence, we do not have any recommendations other than using an icon set that fits to your domain.

Virtual Whiteboards

Virtual whiteboards are usually general-purpose drawing tools with real-time collaboration. We have already mentioned two of their characteristics: First, modeling can become collaborative. Second, whiteboards (analog and digital) tempt users to omit the icons altogether and just use (digital) sticky notes with text (see Figure 5.8).

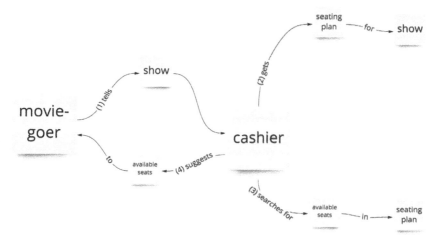

Figure 5.8 *Metropolis 2 without icons on a digital whiteboard*

If that works for you, it's fine. But as we discussed in Chapter 2, "The Pictographic Language," the icons are not just there for beauty; they are supposed to convey meaning, enable discussions, and help with recognition. With a little effort, you can build your own icon set with tools like Miro, Mural, or Conceptboard (see Figure 5.9).

Virtual whiteboards can be combined with other modeling tools. For example, you can upload photos of domain stories that you modeled on an analog whiteboard. That makes it easy to compare several domain stories and annotate them collaboratively. See an example of the result of combining tools in Figure 5.10.

Figure 5.9 *A suggestion for how to use icons in Miro*

Special-Purpose Modeling Tools

In our opinion, a tool that *really* supports Domain Storytelling needs to do the following:

- Enforce the syntactic rules of domain stories. We want a tool for *modeling*, not for *drawing*.

- Number sentences automatically and make it easy to change the sequence of sentences.

- Help with *storytelling* by animating the sequence of sentences.

We built such a modeling tool at our company WPS: *Egon.io—the Domain Story Modeler* (see Figure 5.11). It supports you with numbering and with reorganizing models, and it helps you to retell a story sentence by sentence with a replay mode. If you were wondering how we made the figures in this book, now you know the answer.

Egon.io is open-source. Feel free to use it and adapt it. The source code and a ready-to-use, packaged version are available on GitHub [Egon.io Sources]. Or you can try it online [Egon.io Website].

Choosing a Tool

Table 5.1 lists all the tool categories that we've discussed in this chapter. For each, we recommend a maximum number of participants. Of course, this is not a strict rule.

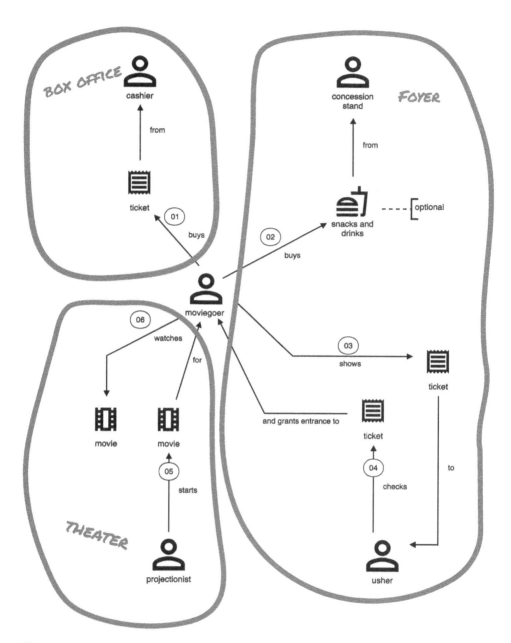

Figure 5.10 *Combining tools—A domain story modeled in Egon.io with groups drawn in Miro*

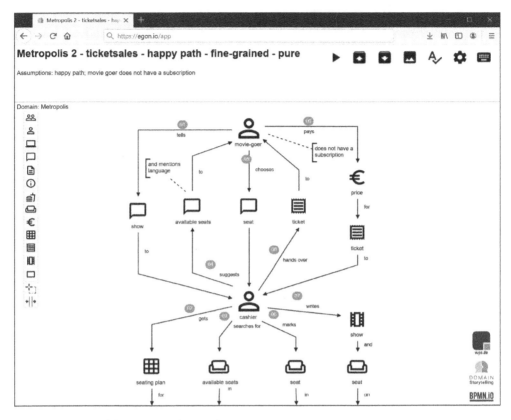

Figure 5.11 *Modeling Metropolis 2 with Egon.io*

Stefan's Flip Chart Story

I once did COARSE-GRAINED Domain Storytelling for finding boundaries (see Chapter 10) with sticky notes on a flip chart with 25 people. It was challenging, and I definitely do not recommend it; but in the end, we reached our goal and then split up into smaller groups for FINE-GRAINED stories.

To help you with deciding which tool to use, we rated how easy it is to correct or restructure a domain story (easy, OK, or hard). We also give recommendations for which tool might be most useful in which situation: spontaneous (little to no preparation required), occasional (familiarity with tool required), and frequent ("enterprise settings" for when you need to create variations of a domain story, compare domain stories, etc.). We also note the degree of modeling support available (enforcing syntactic rules, numbering of activities, and animating the sequence of activities).

Table 5.1 *Comparison of Modeling Tools*

Tool	Group Size	Corrections	Usage	Modeling Support
Sheet of paper	3	Hard	Spontaneous	None
Flip chart (with stickies)	5	Hard	Spontaneous	None
Whiteboard (with stickies)	7	OK	Spontaneous	None
Whiteboard (with kit)	7	OK	Occasional	None
Digitalized hand-drawing	10+	OK	Occasional	None
Drawing tool	10+	Easy	Frequent	None
Virtual whiteboard	10+	Easy	Frequent	None
Egon.io	10+	Easy	Frequent	Good

The tool you choose will have an effect on how the domain story is visualized. In principle, all activities should be numbered so that the number is placed at the origin of the activity's arrow. With some tools it is easier to attach the number to the work object that is used in the activity. (You saw an example for these two variants in Figure 2.16.) There is no intended difference in semantics.

Another thing to consider is that your choice of tool will determine the available space for the model. If you model on flip charts or whiteboards, space is limited. That is not necessarily a disadvantage. Actually, limited modeling space can be helpful to keep domain stories tidy and concise. Digital tools often provide unlimited virtual modeling space and zoom capability. They require a disciplined moderator. As a rule of thumb, a domain story should be limited to the size of the screen (or flip chart, whiteboard, paper) or not more than approximately 20 sentences. If your domain story is much longer than that, consider splitting it into several stories and check if the level of detail is too fine for a visually "verbose" method like Domain Storytelling. We provide some help with splitting stories in Chapter 6, "The Workshop Format."

Chapter 6

The Workshop Format

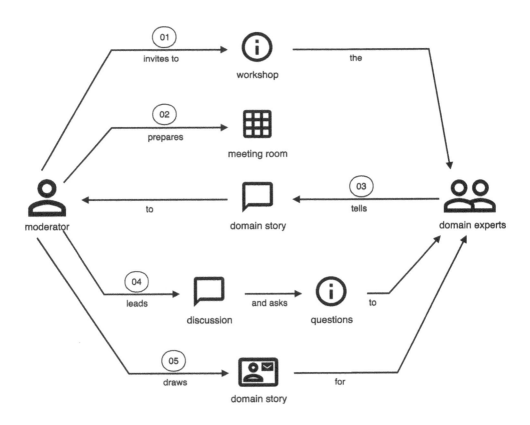

You can use Domain Storytelling just as a graphical notation. But it is much more than that. It is a method for having meaningful conversations about business processes. That's why you typically don't do it on your own. The most important factor is having the right people in the room. When you have the real domain experts in the workshop, with Domain Storytelling you will gain insight into their knowledge.

Domain Storytelling is a conversation technique.

Before the Workshop

The time you can spend with domain experts is usually scarce. A bit of planning may therefore be in order to make the workshop an exciting experience for everyone and to achieve a good result.

The workshop brings together what belongs together: people who want to exchange knowledge using Domain Storytelling for a specific purpose. The purpose is so important that we have dedicated the whole Part II of this book to it. The purpose also determines the granularity of the stories (see Chapter 4, "Scope") and affects the mix of participants.

When we are brought into an organization to moderate a Domain Storytelling workshop, it is usually because one person (from business or IT) has invited us. Let's call that person the **host**. The host is the one who organizes the meeting and invites the participants. The host usually has some idea of what should be modeled. In our experience, however, certain questions and topics will always be important. A moderator can help the host by asking questions like these:

- What questions need to be answered?
- What are the biggest problems?
- Who is involved currently to try to solve these problems?
- Whose perspectives need to be considered? Who should be involved in the host's opinion?
- Which key activities are at the core of the organization?

The host and the moderator should then clarify key activities, use cases, or business processes they want to cover. In a workshop, not just one but several domain stories are told and discussed. Decide what the scope (or scopes; see Chapter 4) of the domain stories should be. The answers to these questions will also help them to choose the right participants.

Inviting the Right Participants

Having the right people present is crucial and therefore needs particularly careful consideration. This is something that Domain Storytelling shares with other collaborative modeling methods.[1]

Who are the right people? In some cases, a single person is able to tell a whole domain story. But usually, nontrivial business processes require cooperation. Several participants should therefore contribute so that the domain story embodies the shared understanding of its narrators.

> Domain Storytelling is usually a collaborative endeavor.

Do not let yourself be limited by organizational boundaries. Especially for domain stories that cover business processes from beginning to end on a COARSE-GRAINED level, there is usually no single person who is an expert on the whole process.

In organizations in which the domain knowledge is divided into silos, it is necessary to invite experts from each silo and get them all to contribute. Gaps and connections between silos will be discovered.

Also, take care to invite real experts—people from the trenches—and not proxies who know the domain from hearsay. Workshop participants generally include the following:

- **Storytellers**—people who can share knowledge (often domain experts from several departments)
- **Listeners**—people who want to learn (often development teams)
- A moderator and a modeler who facilitate the workshop
- The host

In the end, all participants will take away new insights from the workshop, no matter if they were invited to share, to learn, or to facilitate.

---

1. If you are interested in what other authors in the collaborative modeling community suggest, check out Alberto Brandolini's *Introducing EventStorming* [Brandolini 2021] and the *Visual Collaboration Tools* book curated by Kenny Baas-Schwegler and João Rosa [Baas-Schwegler/Rosa 2020].

"Soft" Factors and Politics

Generally, it is better to invite more people than fewer people. You don't want a forgotten expert to curse your workshop like Maleficent in *Sleeping Beauty*. Also, people feel better if they are invited, even if they need to decline that invitation, as opposed to not being invited at all. The moderator should discuss with the host who may be offended if they are not invited.

Having management present at collaborative modeling workshops can be both helpful and problematic, depending on the culture of an organization and the personality of the participants. In some organizations, domain experts will not talk openly about problems when their superiors are present. We have encountered situations where domain experts had to correct superiors or tell them that were not actually following standard procedures, regulations, or company guidelines. Such interactions can only happen in a safe space and require psychological safety, which, unfortunately, not every workplace provides.

If the company itself does not promote open communication and free sharing of ideas, at least you can provide that in the Domain Storytelling workshop.

If you are building a product for many customers, you would usually be faced with a challenge: It would be great to have your customers' view represented in the workshop, but you cannot simply invite a few random customers. In this case, we recommend that you invite a domain expert who works directly with customers (e.g., someone from customer service, sales, etc.) or who has information about customer behavior (e.g., someone from the business intelligence or analytics teams).

In organizations that operate legacy software, the developers who maintain these systems can give valuable input and should be invited to participate. Their views are important not just because they know how to program or administer a database. They sometimes have a more holistic view of the business than domain experts who were trained for years or decades to think within the boundaries of their departments.

How Long Will It Take?

With a little experience, 30–45 minutes can be enough for one COARSE- or FINE-GRAINED AS-IS story. TO-BE stories often take longer, because they are basically design sessions and involve a lot of discussions.

We recommend 60–90 minutes or 2–3 domain stories in 1 session. Continue only after a break or in a follow-up workshop. The length of a workshop would likely be limited by the availability of the people you want to invite. Sessions of two hours, half a day, or a full day can all work, depending on the context.

Preparing the Room

To get a good conversation going, we want to gather people as if around a campfire. For that, we need a pleasant atmosphere and the right setup in the room.

The ideal is the so-called **Stonehenge setup** or **horseshoe setup** (see Figure 6.1): The participants form a circle that is open on one side. This way everybody can see and hear everyone else. From the open side, "the sun will shine in"—that's where the whiteboard or the projection screen (the modeling canvas) goes where the domain stories will be drawn.

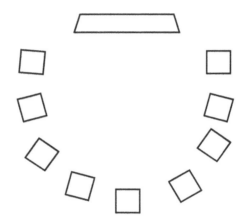

Figure 6.1 *The Stonehenge setup*

People can stand or sit on chairs, beanbags, or whatever your room provides. Tables are not required (and in fact are rather a hinderance). Of course, a table with coffee and cookies makes for a welcome change (especially in companies where people aren't used to being catered to).[2]

It is important that the depicted domain story is always visible to all participants. The number of participants is therefore limited by the visibility of the story. This affects the choice of the tool you use to record the story (see Chapter 5, "Modeling Tools"). If you use a software tool, use a projector to share the moderator's

---

2. On the importance of breaking bread together, consider the pattern "Do Food" in *More Fearless Change* [Manns/Rising 2015].

screen with everyone in the room. Only then is a computer allowed, and only for the moderator.

A remote setting requires different preparation—please see recommendations in the upcoming section "Remote Workshops."

The Workshop

When everybody has found their place and some icebreaking chit-chat has taken place, the moderator opens the actual session. The moderator briefly outlines what is going to happen. This is the right time to clarify the workshop's goals, scope, and content.

Next the moderator explains the **agenda**. We recommend you write it on a flip chart next to the modeling canvas. Typically, the agenda will change during the workshop.

After the introduction, the moderator motivates the participants by asking, "Please tell me your story!"

Storytelling

During the workshop, the moderator needs to steer the storytellers in the right direction to ensure that their contributions serve the overall purpose. Domain experts are not always born storytellers. The crucial prerequisite for good storytelling is a skilled storyteller. That's why the moderator keeps the participants' story going by asking questions like these:

- "What happens next?"
- "Where do you get this information?"
- "How do you determine what to do next?"
- "How do you do that?"

Engage the participants without imposing your opinion on them. Use the language of the participants, not your own!

Sometimes, activities seem to lack an obvious purpose. It is important to understand *why* activities are carried out in order to later design useful software and processes (see Chapter 11, "Working with Requirements"). The answer as to why something is done a certain way often reveals serious problems with current processes or how they are supported by software:

- "That is the way we have always done it."
- "I don't know why we do that."
- "We have been assuming that this is necessary for the folks from the other department."
- "Because the software forces us to do it this way."

You might have to ask *why* repeatedly to get to the bottom of the problem.

Graphical Recording

As the participants tell their story, the moderator records it graphically—step-by-step, thus determining the pace of the storytelling. While recording, the moderator should retell the sentence that they are modeling. To make sure that the actual terms from the domain language are used, confirm by asking, "Is this the right term?"

> The moderator repeats in a visual way what they have understood from the participant's story.

In addition, the moderator should introduce an icon when it first appears in the story: "I will use this receipt icon to represent the ticket." The participants see what gets recorded and can give immediate feedback. Most of the story should be presented in the pictographic language, with some textual annotations—not the other way round!

Try to avoid plot holes in the story—identifiable by parts that are not connected by arrows (see Figure 6.2).

You can see that the story in Figure 6.2 jumps from the moviegoer to the usher. How does the usher get the ticket? Is the ticket checked before or after the moviegoer enters the building? With some experience, you will come to realize that the pictographic language helps you to ask the right questions: "Who does this?" "How do they know that they have to do this now?" "How do the actors communicate with each other?"

When participants tell their story, they are likely to complain about something: "This goes wrong all the time!" "We have had this problem for years!" Although this is not exactly part of the story, it is valuable information that is worth making a note of. If you have chosen a whiteboard with sticky notes, use a sticky note in a different color to highlight pain points.

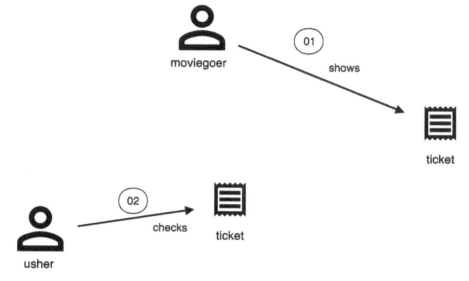

Figure 6.2 *Don't: Leave plot holes between the sentences of a domain story*

 Make pain points visible by annotations.

It is also important to check that the scope of the story is consistent (see Chapter 4).

When You Are Stuck

This section addresses obstacles and how to overcome them.

If you get stuck right at the beginning, consider starting the story differently. Try to replace the beginning of the story with an assumption. In the cinema example, you could suggest: "Let's assume that you have already decided which movie you want to see. How do you buy the tickets?"

There are some common pitfalls that will make you feel like you've lost control of the story:

- Are you mixing story lines? Stick to the story—there should always be just one story line.

- Are you mixing AS-IS and TO-BE processes? Decide what you want to model and focus on that.

- Are you having trouble dealing with objections, alternatives, and ideas for improvements? Use annotations to get them out of the way. Make it clear to the other participants that they need to focus on one story line and that you will go through the collected annotations later.

When the storytelling hits a dead end, it can be helpful to remind everyone of the purpose of the workshop. Remind them why you chose the particular scenario. Revisit your assumptions. Then, tell the participants the story from the beginning, sentence by sentence.

Another source of trouble are participants who cannot agree on anything. In such cases, we have found it useful to make the stories more concrete by naming actors with people's names instead of their role. This clarifies that the story is told from one person's point of view. For example: The Metropolis employs two cashiers—Charlotte and Carlos—who sell tickets in completely different ways. Instead of modeling both Charlotte and Carlos as "cashier," start with, e.g., Charlotte and use her name for the actor. Then ask Carlos how his version of the process is different from Charlotte's version. Making differences visible is a good first step toward resolving them.

As the moderator, you also have to ask yourself if Domain Storytelling is the right modeling method for the job. Use it if you think it will help with the goal you are trying to achieve. Do not use it blindly because it has been useful to you in the past, because it's new, or because it's the only modeling method you have experience with. If you come across a situation where you are having difficulty using Domain Storytelling, ask yourself what is causing it:

- Is it a problem with the domain itself (e.g., it is inherently hard to understand)?
- Is it a problem with your modeling skills?

If you can answer both questions with "no," you are probably trying to use Domain Storytelling for something that it should not be used for. We want to encourage you to learn more techniques of collaborative modeling and facilitation. Some of them we will briefly describe in Chapter 7, "Relationships to Other Modeling Methods." It can also be useful to look at techniques from the design world (such as mockups). Also, *Liberating Structures* can help with problem-solving, decision-making, planning, and feedback [LiberatingStructures Website].

When the Story Gets Too Big

Depending on the modeling tool, the potential length of a story might be limited. As a rule of thumb, the following limits apply:

- **Flip chart:** 10 sentences

- **Large whiteboard:** 15 sentences
- **Digital tools:** 20 sentences

In some situations, we have exceeded the limits. But at a certain point, the visual recording becomes too cluttered, unmanageable, or hard to grasp. See, for example, Metropolis 5 in Figure 6.3: If you open the model in Egon.io and use its replay-function, the story is still manageable. But if you want to use the picture in books or presentations, it is worth considering splitting the domain story into shorter ones.

Here are some strategies for dealing with big stories:

- Change to a more COARSE-GRAINED scope, especially if you have not grasped the big picture yet.

- Thin the plot: Choose an easier story line or avoid side plots.

- Use assumptions to skip the first few steps of the story. In Metropolis 2 (see Figure 1.10), for example, instead of modeling how a moviegoer chooses the movie they want to see, write an annotation: "We assume the moviegoer has already chosen which movie to see and there are shows that fit their time."

- Split one story into several stories: If none of the previous strategies works for you, it might be because your story requires a certain depth and cannot be thinned or aggregated. Still, you can split it into several stories. Try to cut the story after an intermediate result is reached, or use a handover of a work object as the last sentence of one story and the first sentence of another story. When the story line moves from one subdomain to another or from one department to another, that is also a good place for a story split. Please keep in mind that cliffhangers are exciting when they happen in your favorite TV series, but not in a domain story.

How to Create the Right Atmosphere

As a moderator, you can take certain measures to create a productive atmosphere.

Keep an Eye on Your Participants

- Does someone dominate the conversation and need to be reminded of boundaries?

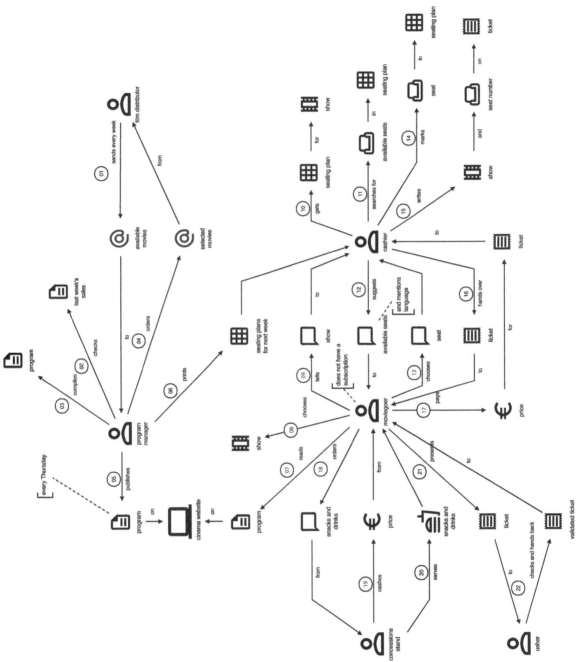

Figure 6.3 *Too long for books and presentations: Metropolis 5*

- Who is silent/shy/uncomfortable and needs encouragement?
- Who is reluctant to speak and needs to get something off their chest?

Establish Rules

Be open, be honest, be respectful.
—Code of Conduct, CoMoCamp [CoMoCamp Website]

As we said before, polite manners are easily forgotten in a heated discussion. Therefore, it can be useful to establish some basic rules or a code of conduct. Here are some ideas:

- Let others finish their sentences.
- Treat each other respectfully.
- When discussing problems, do not blame each other.
- Be truthful to the best of your knowledge.

Stay in Control

Even with a code of conduct in place, you should watch out for people who pose a threat to a productive atmosphere:

- Attention seekers who see collaborative modeling as a chance to boast about how great they are.
- Frustrated people who treat collaborative modeling as a chance to let off steam.
- Managers who used to be domain experts before they got promoted to management and have since lost touch with the domain.

Even for experienced moderators, situations like these are difficult to handle. But it is your responsibility to achieve a good result. Hence, you have to intervene:

- Make it clear that for a good result all perspectives must be considered, not just the managers' or longest-serving employees' opinions.
- Emphasize the goal of the workshop and the time frame you are working with. Postpone discussions that are out of scope.

Provide a "parking lot"—a visual space for postponed discussions and ideas so that you can revisit them later.

Finishing a Domain Story

When the story seems to be finished, tell the story from the beginning and try to get agreement: Did we miss something? Is something obviously wrong? Do all domain experts agree with the story? Revisit the annotations for possible alternative stories. Let the participants decide which ones are minor variations and which deserve their own domain story. As a moderator, you can stimulate this discussion with questions like these:

- Are we talking about the same task that is sometimes done differently? Or are we talking about a different task?
- What would be different if…?
- Am I right that the only difference would be…?

If necessary, model another domain story. Maybe you'll want to schedule a follow-up workshop to take a more detailed look at parts of the story or to deal with important variations. If everything went right, you have now built a common understanding about a relevant part of the domain. However, you will rarely succeed 100% in bringing the views of several people to one common denominator. Be careful not to jump to abstractions in order to avoid conflicting views. Instead, use annotations to bring unresolvable differences to everyone's attention.

If something seems noteworthy, make it explicit.

Write it down as an annotation. Then, people can see it, can point to it, can object to it. Making things visible adds quality to the discussion.

After the Workshop

When the workshop is finished, the result should be documented. Take a picture of the whiteboard. If you drew the picture with a tool, it is good practice to tidy up the model to reduce clutter. Then, share the picture or file. Note, however, that the visualization of a domain story was not intended to be a stand-alone document. First and foremost, the picture is for the people who are telling the story while they are telling it. Later, it will serve as a memory aid for those who participated in the workshop and for telling the story to other people.

Other artifacts of the software development process will crystallize and grow around the domain stories as well. Take, for example, *context maps* (see Chapter 10, "Finding Boundaries"), written *requirements* (see Chapter 11, "Working with Requirements"), and the *code model*[3] (see Chapter 12, "Modeling in Code"). You can also continue the conversation about the domain with the help of other modeling techniques, such as Example Mapping [Wynne 2015] and EventStorming [Brandolini 2021].

> The act of modeling is often more important than the actual model.

If you missed the workshop, you missed the "campfire" experience. Looking at a finished domain story is not the same as participating in the making of it, because Domain Storytelling is a *collaborative learning experience*. The participants reflect on their own day-to-day work and learn from their colleagues how they perceive the domain in a different way.

To-Be Workshops

In the spirit of collaborative modeling, we see process design as a collaborative activity in the form of workshops. In a TO-BE workshop, several things have to be done differently than in AS-IS modeling.

When modeling AS-IS processes, you are mainly *analyzing*. You look at the world through your domain experts' eyes and describe it as these experts perceive it (as well as you can). You are focused on the present and explore the problem space. The main goal is understanding.

With TO-BE processes, on the other hand, you will find yourself in the solution space and in the future. Also, you are not analyzing, but *constructively designing*— usually on the basis of a previously analyzed problem space. That means you look at the world and describe how it will be (or how you hope it will be). This usually includes some sort of improvements and process changes, especially if the TO-BE process will be implemented through software. After all, you do not want to just re-implement a bad AS-IS process. For more on that topic, see Chapter 13, "Supporting Organizational Change."

---

3. In the end, the code is the model, and the model is the code.

> While analysis is about something that already exists, design creates something that is new.

When preparing for a TO-BE workshop, keep in mind the following:

- TO-BE domain stories usually take longer to tell and record than AS-IS stories. We recommend you allocate 50% more time.
- Be prepared for a lot more discussion compared to an AS-IS workshop.
- Come ready to use other workshop techniques that complement Domain Storytelling, e.g., to collect feedback on a proposed process improvement (see the upcoming section "The Moderator").

What can you do as a moderator to facilitate a successful TO-BE workshop? Here are our recommendations:

- **Avoid confusion by talking about a specific point in time:** Define the point in the future when the TO-BE processes take place. It makes a big difference if one of the participants thinks of the future in 6 months and another one thinks of the future in 24 months.
- **Do not settle for the first result:** Model and compare different variants of the future process (for the same point in time).
- **Make room for improvements:** As a moderator, you need to challenge the participants' story more rigorously. Question every sentence to uncover hidden assumptions. For example, ask "why" again and again to discover the purpose of a proposed activity (or the lack thereof).
- **Free the participants' minds from current system boundaries:** Instead of using the names of existing systems as actors, use fictional names that describe their job (like "a system that schedules marketing campaigns") or placeholders (like "System X," "System Y," "System Z").
- **Free the participants' minds from current roles and responsibilities:** Instead of existing roles and job titles, use fictional names and placeholders for human actors.
- **Challenge the scope of the proposed software systems:** Ask if the TO-BE process would lead to a tight coupling of software systems—meaning, is a system

able to fulfill a task only if it cooperates closely with another system? That would be bad, of course!

- **Challenge the proposed processes:** Try to re-enact concrete examples from the past with the TO-BE domain stories. Can the proposed process handle the examples?

Remote Workshops

Domain Storytelling was conceived for on-site workshops. We have since found that it also works well in remote settings if you take into account a few things:

- All participants need to be able to see the visual representation of the domain story (in real time, as it evolves).

- All participants need to be able to hear each other.

The first point requires a digital modeling tool and screen sharing. If the modeling tool doesn't already have this capability, you should use a videoconferencing software. We have used the combination of videoconferencing and Egon.io or virtual whiteboards (see Chapter 5, "Modeling Tools") successfully.

In addition to the previous two requirements, we have some recommendations:

- Use video (not just audio) and ask all participants to do the same. Seeing the participants enables you to read at least some body language. A setup with two screens (one for the video feed and one for the modeling tool) is helpful.

- Split the roles of moderator and modeler, especially for larger groups. The moderator can focus on the participants. Handling a group of people can be difficult even if everyone is in the same room. Dealing with muted microphones and people cutting each other off makes the moderator's task even more challenging in a virtual setting.

- Set a timer for a short modeling session (around 45 minutes) followed by a break. This helps people to stay focused. Try to tell a story from beginning to end within the time frame.

- The experience is usually smoother if the participants and the moderator/modeler are already familiar with one another. Then the information loss (body language, interpersonal relationships) that occurs in a remote setting is less of a problem.

- For important workshops, do a pre-event check to ensure all participants are comfortable with the software used.

Our impressions so far are mixed: While remote workshops can encourage some participants to ask more questions, others are more reluctant to give negative feedback. Perhaps these are side effects of not being fully immersed in the workshop. After all, it is so easy to get distracted when one is at the computer. A moderator can help the participants to keep (or regain) their focus by retelling the domain story from time to time. In addition, the moderator should request feedback frequently.

If you follow these recommendations, you will be able to run successful remote workshops. The spirit of Domain Storytelling can easily be carried over from on-site to virtual settings.[4]

The Moderator

The moderator's responsibility is to bring together storytellers and listeners and help them to create a shared understanding.

Facilitating a workshop may sometimes be challenging, but it can be learned. In this section, we have compiled some advice for moderators. In our experience, moderating workshops can be incredibly rewarding and is worth the effort.

Who Can Play the Role?

The role of the **moderator** stands out. It can be played by a neutral facilitator with no prior knowledge of the domain and with no other intention than helping the participants. A Scrum master, agile coach, or external consultant can be a good fit for this position.

However, the moderator role is often assumed by the host (the person who has initiated the workshop and invited people to participate) or a listener. As a product owner, software developer, or business analyst, they want to learn about the domain and its business processes. Staying neutral as a moderator is usually a concern when you are in the problem space. When moving on to the solution space, moderators may give advice on how to optimize the process and use new technologies.

---

4. You can watch Stefan do a remote modeling session on YouTube [Hofer 2020]. Even though this video shows a session with just one domain expert and one moderator, it gives you an idea of how it is meant to work.

There is, however, another possibility. The moderator could also be one of the storytellers. In this case, the moderator needs to be careful not to forget their primary responsibility. They might be tempted to steer the conversation into a direction that they prefer. This is risky because it undermines the purpose of the workshop. It also damages the credibility of the moderator, making it harder for them to resolve conflicts.

In summary, the moderator could be the following:

- A neutral person
- The host or another listener
- A storyteller

Learning to Facilitate

Some things are better done than described... Here's a challenge for you. Write a short description that tells someone how to tie bows in their shoelaces.
—The Pragmatic Programmers [Hunt/Thomas 1999]

By now, you have read a lot about Domain Storytelling. Maybe you have also seen a video recording of one of our tutorials. But reading and watching on their own don't make you a practitioner; you need to *practice*. We recommend the following.

First, try it on your own. Pen and paper are all the tools you need. Model a process that you are familiar with. Here are some ideas:

- Having dinner at a restaurant
- Buying groceries
- Going on holiday
- Electing the government of your country

Focus on the pictographic language. Get familiar with the way a story is visualized. Experiment with variations of your process: What if you model the variation as a separate domain story? Or can you capture it as a textual annotation?

The next step is to ask a friend or a friendly colleague for help. Grab a whiteboard or a flip chart, some sticky notes, and a marker. Have the friend tell you a story that they are an expert in. Focus on being a moderator: How do you motivate your domain expert toward intensive cooperation? Can you keep up visualizing the domain story while listening and asking questions? Try to capture your expert's point of view and not your own. Learn how to avoid making implicit assumptions or drawing premature conclusions.

Then, think of a real-world problem that you have encountered and that can be explored with Domain Storytelling. Ideally, pick something that can be discussed with a small group of domain experts. Focus on managing the group and turning their individual stories into one domain story that everyone can agree on.

The Modeler as Separate Role

Since moderating and modeling are demanding tasks, we recommend beginners separate the role of the *moderator* from the role of the *modeler*. One person assumes the role of the moderator and is responsible for managing the domain experts. Another person becomes the **modeler** and captures the domain story. To make that work, both need to be familiar with the method. They also need to communicate well and support each other. For example, the storytelling needs to move at the same speed as the visualization.

For large workshops and heated discussions, we would also recommend splitting the tasks so that one person can focus on moderating, and the other person can focus on modeling.

If you are the modeler, you should keep in mind that modeling is not about (software) tools. They are there only to support you and should not distract the participants.

The more experience you gain with modeling domain stories, the more relaxed you will be about the grammar of the pictographic language that we described in Chapter 2, "The Pictographic Language." Once you know what a domain story should look like, the training wheels can be taken off. After all, the point is to convey meaning, not to follow strict rules. Of course, we are not encouraging you to throw everything we have written out the window. But at some point you should start treating it as advice, not as law.

Moderated Mode vs. Co-Op Mode

If you work with a small group of participants who are already familiar with Domain Storytelling, modeling can be a collaborative activity that includes all participants (**co-op mode**). Such a setup can be more fun than having designated moderators/modelers who do all the modeling (**moderated mode**).

If the participants are not used to the Domain Storytelling way of reasoning about workflows, shared modeling responsibilities can lead to a chaotic workshop that will make the moderator's life hard. There is a good chance that you'll end up with an incoherent model or a model that reflects the view of the loudest participant. Thus, working in co-op mode requires a few agreed upon guardrails: which scenario the domain story is about, which icons to use for the pictographic language, and which scope to aim for.

Whether distributing modeling tasks is an option for you will also depend on the tool you use to visualize the story (see Chapter 5, "Modeling Tools"). To enable it, you'd need everyone to have access to the canvas and the ability to change the model.

Chapter 7

Relationship to Other Modeling Methods

Domain Storytelling is best perceived as another tool in your modeling toolbox. This chapter covers some other methods that also belong in this toolbox and can be combined with Domain Storytelling. There are situations where you can use them interchangeably, and there are situations where one fits better than the other. And then, there are situations where it makes sense to combine these techniques to tackle specific modeling problems.

> This chapter reflects our views and experience. We want to encourage you to build your own toolbox.

Domain-Driven Design

The first method we refer to is actually not a modeling method in the narrower sense of the term but an approach that deals with the development of business software: *Domain-Driven Design (DDD)* [Evans 2004].

DDD does not describe a single modeling method, but it emphasizes collaborative modeling by domain experts and development teams as the essential part of software development. It is the foundation for the following:

- *Strategic design*: The more details you learn and model about a domain, the more complex and confusing the models become. To avoid that, DDD suggests to subdivide the domain into bounded contexts. Each bounded context has its own model of the domain and its own domain language. A bounded context is a stable foundation on which to build software. Collaborative modeling helps with finding boundaries between bounded contexts and modeling the details within them.

- *Tactical design*: Domain experts and development teams work hard to design domain models in their heads and in diagrams. But why stop before the code level? DDD provides technical guidance (so-called *building blocks*) on how to represent different concepts of a domain in code. Teams use collaborative modeling to figure out which concepts of the domain can best be implemented with which building blocks.

- *Ubiquitous language*: This language is derived from the domain language and is consistent within a bounded context. This language should be used everywhere (ubiquitously)—from the spoken words of the domain expert to the whiteboard to the code. Keep in mind that there are usually several ubiquitous languages in a company (one per bounded context). It is not a uniform, company-wide language.

If this has sparked your curiosity about DDD, here are some recommended introductory readings:

- Vaughn Vernon's *Domain-Driven Design Distilled* is a great and concise introduction to DDD [Vernon 2016].[1]
- Scott Millet's *The Anatomy of Domain-Driven Design* sums up DDD on 24 illustrated pages [Millet 2017].

How to Combine DDD with Domain Storytelling

If you already have experience with DDD, you will have realized by now that the general ideas behind Domain Storytelling fit well into a DDD mindset: It is a concrete way of implementing collaborative modeling by domain experts and development teams.

Furthermore, in Part II of this book we will describe specific purposes of Domain Storytelling that are particularly useful in the context of DDD:

- Learning domain language for developing a ubiquitous language (see Chapter 9).

---

1. Henning helped to translate the book from English to German: *Domain-Driven Design kompakt* [Vernon 2017].

- Finding boundaries for strategic design (see Chapter 10).
- Modeling in code for tactical design (see Chapter 12).

EventStorming

EventStorming [Brandolini 2021] is a collaborative modeling method that was developed in the context of DDD. During an EventStorming workshop, developers and experts from various departments use sticky notes to create a picture of complex business processes. This picture is created bottom-up by writing domain events on the sticky notes and placing them on a timeline from left to right. After a deliberately chaotic start (hence "storming"), a story emerges, captured as a flow of events that are relevant to the domain experts.

For the Metropolis movie theater, during an EventStorming the modeling space might look like in Figure 7.1—a timeline of domain events on orange sticky notes.[2]

Figure 7.1 *Metropolis big-picture EventStorming*

This style of EventStorming is called *big picture*. By adding some notational elements, it can be elaborated into a detailed process model and into a software design model. Such modeling works well if software is to be built according to DDD.

Similarities and Differences

Both Domain Storytelling and EventStorming focus on close collaboration with the domain experts. A major difference is that EventStorming places events on a timeline and Domain Storytelling shows the cooperation between actors. While an event

---

2. For production reasons, while the e-book edition of this book contains colors, the print edition uses grayscale instead.

storm shows what's happening, a domain story shows who is doing what with whom.

EventStorming starts with a chaotic storming phase followed by consolidation. In Domain Storytelling, we have much smaller iterations of storming (discussing the next sentence) and consolidation (recording that sentence).

Another difference is that with EventStorming you can visualize several scenarios in one picture (often, the story lines are arranged in lanes so that they do not get mixed up), while a domain story is about only one particular scenario. However, many people use a scenario-based form of EventStorming with a single flow of events, which of course is similar to the Domain Storytelling approach.

The methods differ in how workshops are typically facilitated. With Domain Storytelling, you have a moderator who channels the participants' input by modeling it. With EventStorming, the participants storm a scenario. However, things are not as black and white as they seem. Domain Storytelling can be used in a cooperative mode (see Chapter 6, "The Workshop Format"), and some EventStorming practitioners switch to a single-modeler mode if needed.

Here are some situations in which we use EventStorming:

- If the domain is not very structured, EventStorming's brainstorming approach can be preferable to a sentence-by-sentence and beginning-to-end approach.

- If the domain is characterized by time-related processes and status changes, an approach that focuses on a timeline of events seems a natural fit.

- If we want to model a highly detailed scenario using single-flow EventStorming, then the notation scales more easily. Dozens or hundreds of events are easier to handle with EventStorming than the same number of sentences in Domain Storytelling.

Here are some situations in which we prefer Domain Storytelling:

- If the domain involves many actors (people or software).

- If we want to investigate how actors communicate and cooperate with each other.

- When TO-BE processes are to be designed, a common perspective emerges more easily from a moderated, sentence-by-sentence approach.

- If creating documentation is a goal.

- When the corporate culture is more suited to a moderated, structured approach rather than EventStorming's brainstorming approach.

How to Combine EventStorming with Domain Storytelling

Both EventStorming and Domain Storytelling can be applied at different levels of detail and to AS-IS and TO-BE processes. Hence, there are a lot of possible combinations. We have tried some of them successfully:

From EventStorming to Domain Storytelling

In big-picture EventStorming, you might come across parts of the process that are cooperative, i.e., several people or systems are actively involved. If these parts are critical to your analysis of a domain, you might want to go the extra mile to get another perspective on the process: You can model the cooperative part of the process additionally as a domain story.

From Domain Storytelling to EventStorming

In Chapter 12, "Modeling in Code," we will show you how to turn FINE-GRAINED domain stories into source code. This task is also addressed by EventStorming at the so-called *design level*. The notational elements on that level fit very well to the implementation styles *Command-Query Responsibility Segregation* (*CQRS*, [Young 2010]) and *Event Sourcing* [Fowler 2005]. If you are familiar with this flavor of EventStorming, you can use it as a follow-up to COARSE-GRAINED domain stories.

User Story Mapping

User Story Mapping [Patton 2014] comes from the agile community. This simple and versatile method primarily aims to improve product development. It helps you to structure requirements into a coherent story from the users' perspective. On sticky notes or cards, the participants briefly describe how they imagine interacting with the software. These cards or notes represent *user stories* [Cohn 2004] and are placed on a wall to form a two-dimensional map (hence the name of the method). The horizontal dimension of a user story map depicts a business process or a user journey. The vertical dimension is used for detailing requirements and prioritization.

At the Metropolis, app developer Anna and movie theater manager Matthew modeled a domain story that shows how cashiers will sell tickets using a new box-office app. Figure 7.2 shows a first, rudimentary *user story map* for the box-office app.

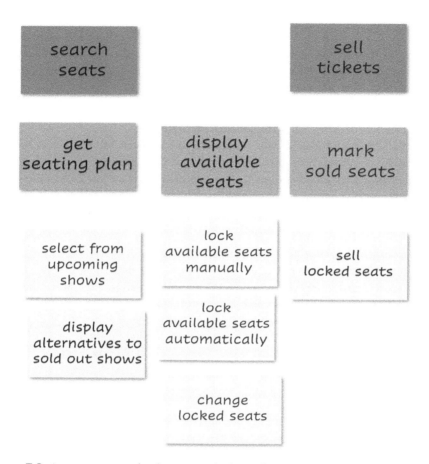

Figure 7.2 *A user story map for the Metropolis box-office app*

The user story map is used as a planning instrument for cross-functional agile teams to do the following:

- Talk to a product owner about priorities and increments
- Not lose sight of the context of a user story
- Clarify which requirements need to be worked out in detail next

We have found that a user story map prevents teams from falling into the "flat backlog trap" [Patton 2014]: If a backlog contains dozens or hundreds of requirements, teams lose perspective of how these requirements form a useful product. User story maps provide context to the requirements, thus making it easier to prioritize and slice them.

Similarities and Differences

Both methods are about telling stories. Also, both methods allow you to tell stories at different levels of detail and with different scopes. While a domain story (and similarly a user story) focuses on a particular granularity, a user story map shows different granularities at once. What we call AS-IS and TO-BE in domain stories are called the *now story map* and the *later story map* in User Story Mapping.

The two methods differ a lot in the way that stories are captured visually. A story map doesn't show how the actors in a story interact. However, User Story Mapping has its strengths when it comes to planning the implementation of requirements.

If you are familiar with User Story Mapping, please note that both Domain Storytelling and User Story Mapping use the term *activity*, but they don't necessarily mean the same thing.

How to Combine User Story Mapping with Domain Storytelling

We have frequently used User Story Mapping as a follow-up to Domain Storytelling. Once the TO-BE processes have reached a certain maturity, we want to derive requirements. User Story Mapping then helps us to transfer the requirements to a structured backlog. In Chapter 11, "Working with Requirements," we will describe this in detail and give an example.

When a user story is sprint ready and moves on from product backlog to sprint backlog, FINE-GRAINED domain stories are often the right tool for finding out how to implement that user story. They are especially helpful with building the domain model. We will describe how this is done in Chapter 12, "Modeling in Code."

Example Mapping

Example Mapping [Wynne 2015] facilitates discussions about software requirements. It is used by development teams before they start implementing a requirement to clarify the acceptance criteria of a requirement. The Example Mapping method was developed in the context of BDD [North 2006].

In an Example Mapping workshop, user stories are the starting point for understanding the problem domain in more detail. Concrete instances of a user story serve as *examples*. Using these examples, representatives of the business department, developers, and testers in particular identify the business rules or boundary conditions of a user story in order to derive acceptance tests. User stories, rules with examples, and open questions are each written down on cards of different colors to capture the conversation.

Figure 7.3 shows an Example Mapping session at the Metropolis. Matthew and Anna are in the process of clarifying the user story "Lock available seats automatically" they had discovered during Domain Storytelling and User Story Mapping (see Figure 7.2 and first row in Figure 7.3). Matthew's initial rules (second row in Figure 7.3) for the requirement are challenged by concrete examples (third and fourth rows in Figure 7.3).

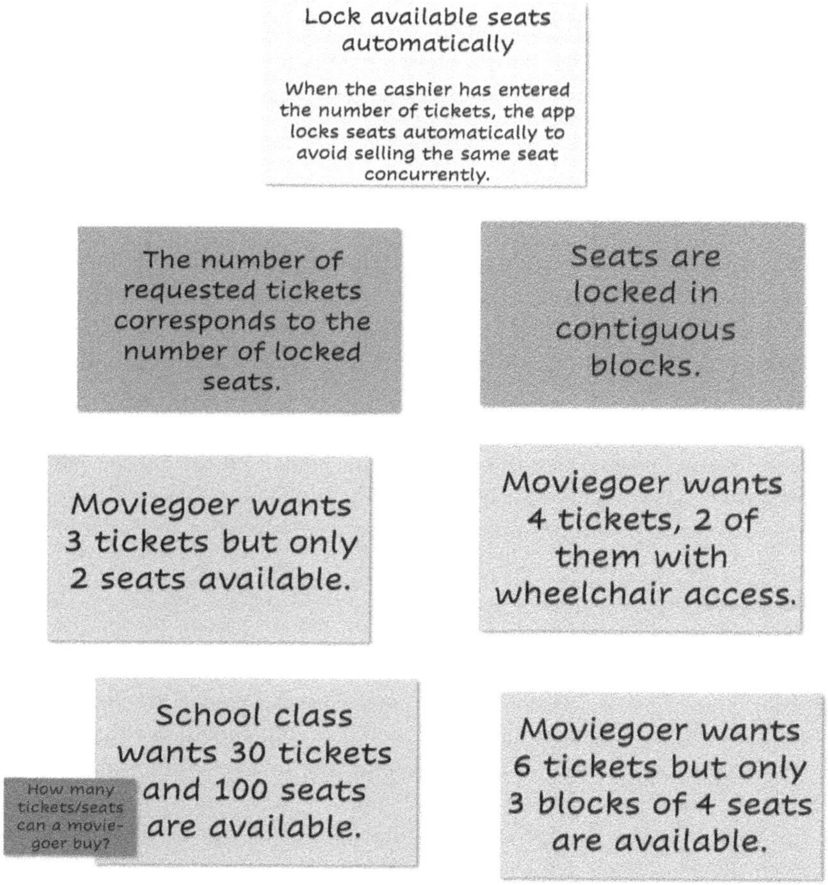

Figure 7.3 *An Example Map for the Metropolis box-office app*

Similarities and Differences

There is not much overlap between Example Mapping and Domain Storytelling as they focus on different aspects of the domain: A domain story visualizes one concrete path of a business process. Example Mapping is about exploring what is to the left and right of that path. With Example Mapping, you keep asking "What else could happen?" and "What makes this case different from other cases?" Hence, the two techniques complement each other very well.

How to Combine Example Mapping with Domain Storytelling

You can either go directly from domain stories to an example map, or—like in Figure 7.3—use it as third step after Domain Storytelling and User Story Mapping. With Example Mapping, we continue to work on FINE-GRAINED domain stories in the following cases:

- When we need to analyze the business rules that determine process variants
- To detail the requirements to an implementable level
- If it becomes clear during planning that requirements need to be cut into smaller pieces

Storystorming

The goal of Storystorming is to provide a consistent approach from business goals and business strategy to the implementation level [Schimak 2019]. To achieve that, it draws ideas from DDD, BDD, and agile software development. It integrates several existing modeling techniques and aligns their notations; therefore, modelers can move from one technique to the next more easily. Currently, Storystorming features EventStorming, User Story Mapping, Impact Mapping—and Domain Storytelling. However, Storystorming puts a twist on Domain Storytelling: To align with other approaches, the notation is replaced by Storystorming's color-coded sticky notes notation. This version of Domain Storytelling is simply referred to as *storytelling*.

Similarities and Differences

We will focus here on the storytelling part of Storystorming. An obvious difference is of course the notation. To give you an idea, we modeled the domain story Metropolis 1 depicted in Figure 1.9 using the Storystorming notation in Figure 7.4.

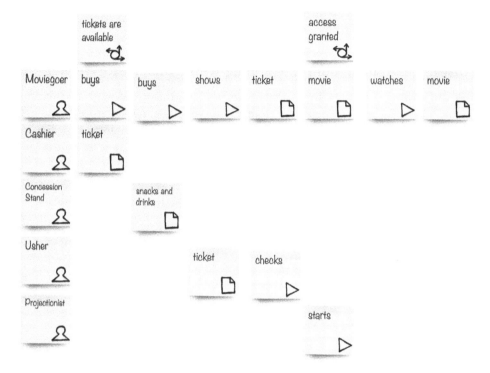

Figure 7.4 *Metropolis 1 in Storystorming notation*

To understand the notation, please see the legend depicted in Figure 7.5 and following explanation:

- Each lane represents an actor and their actions. The actor sticky is put on the left side, at the beginning of the lane. Human actors are put on a yellow sticky with a stick figure icon (e.g., "moviegoer"). Machine actors are put on a pink sticky with a computer icon.

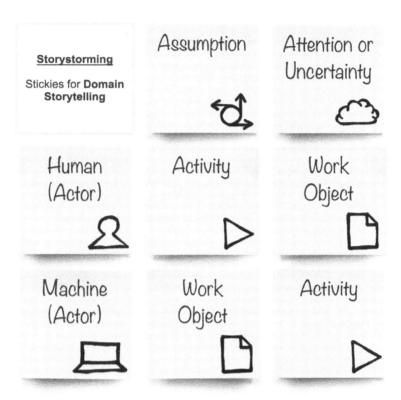

Figure 7.5 *Storystorming legend*

- The activity (blue sticky with play button icon) is always placed into the lane of the actor. The work object (green sticky with document icon) is placed on the lane of the secondary actor (e.g., activity "buys" with work object "ticket"). If there is no other actor involved, the work object is put on the lane of the actor (e.g., activity "watches" with work object "movie").

- The sentences of the story are always read from blue/play button icon (verb) to green/document icon (object).

- An assumption (purple sticky with arrow circle icon) that is expressed by a sentence is put above that sentence, e.g., "tickets are available."

If you read the Storystorming model and the domain story of the Metropolis 1 scenario out loud, they will sound similar. Still, the two alternative notations have their pros and cons:

- To use a textual notation with color-coded sticky notes, all you need is a (virtual) whiteboard and sticky notes. For a pictographic language with numbered arrows, a whiteboard may suffice, but additional tooling speeds up the modeling.

- A domain story's layout is flexible, enabling modelers to express additional information by rearranging sentences and grouping them together. Storystorming's layout is based on a grid. On the one hand, this is less flexible. On the other hand, it makes it easier to find the next sentence and renders sequence numbers obsolete.

- The pictographic language can convey additional semantics, and discussing which icon represents a work object can generate interesting insights. However, sometimes finding the right icon can be time-consuming and distracting.

- Using sticky notes may lower the barrier for cooperative modeling (without a designated modeler).

- Storystorming makes it easy to map concepts from other methods (like *events* and *deliverables*) to the story.

How to Combine Storystorming with Domain Storytelling

As of the writing of this book, Storystorming is still a relatively new method. We have not had the opportunity to get enough practical experience with it to suggest how it can best be combined with Domain Storytelling (or whether it makes sense to combine them at all). However, we think it is an interesting approach to storytelling and worth a second look.

Use Cases

Basically, a use case is a textual description of a sequence of steps a user of a system takes to reach a certain goal. In other words, a use case describes a scenario. Although use cases are not a visual modeling method, we included them in this chapter because they are relevant to Domain Storytelling and to domain modeling in general.

Originally introduced by Ivar Jacobson at OOPLSA '87 [Jacobson 1987], several styles of use cases have developed. Alistair Cockburn's styles from *Writing Effective Use Cases* [Cockburn 2001] are probably the most influential ones.

The level of detail and degree of formality vary from style to style. For example, Cockburn's *fully dressed* style consists of a main success scenario, preconditions, triggers, scope, primary actors, and so on.

Similarities and Differences

Jacobson made storytelling one of the main principles of use cases ("Keep it simple by telling stories" [Jacobson et al. 2011]). Domain Storytelling is a great way to implement this principle in order to identify the main success scenario (also called the *basic flow*) and collect alternative flows. Once the story is told and visualized, a use cases template can be used to write down the flows as text and add important additional information. Hence, use cases and domain stories complement each other very well.

How to Combine Use Cases with Domain Storytelling

The origins of Domain Storytelling go back to the heyday of use cases, so it is not surprising that the use case format was used to document the results of a Domain Storytelling workshop. We still recommend it when domain stories are shared as text and pictures rather than as a conversation, e.g., as part of a tender. Further on, we will show the transition from business processes to requirements with user stories and User Story Mapping.

Even if you do not intend to document your domain stories, take a look at some use case templates. They are quite useful as a checklist for a Domain Storytelling conversation.

UML

The *Unified Modeling Language (UML)* is a primarily graphical notation used to support object-oriented modeling [Rumbaugh et al. 2005]. It has become groundbreaking for modeling and software development. We assume that our readers are at least somewhat familiar with it.

Similarities and Differences

For us, UML is first of all a medium for communication between developers. Domain Storytelling, on the other hand, is mostly a medium for communication between developer and domain expert.

There are some similarities between domain stories and UML *behavior diagrams*. *Activity diagrams* and *sequence diagrams* define a notation for processes. Sequence diagrams are also scenario-based, like domain stories.

How to Combine UML with Domain Storytelling

When we are dealing with many domain stories, we sometimes use UML *use case diagrams* as an overview. The notation of use case diagrams contains *actors*, so there is a direct connection to domain stories. In a use case diagram, you can collect all actors that play a role in your domain stories. The use cases in the diagram then show which scenarios are modeled as domain stories. In Chapter 3, "Scenario-Based Modeling," you have seen an example of a use case diagram that provided an overview of the Metropolis cinema in Figure 3.5.

From FINE-GRAINED domain stories a domain model can be extracted. A good way to express this model is as a UML *class diagram*. We will show how this is done in Chapter 12, "Modeling in Code."

BPMN

Business Process Model and Notation (BPMN) is a graphical representation for modeling business processes [OMG 2013]. Like UML, it can be used in a formal way to describe processes that are then executed by a process engine. It is also widely used in a nonexecutable way to document and analyze business processes.

Similarities and Differences

While Domain Storytelling is scenario-based, which means that each domain story focuses on one instance of a business process, a BPMN model can contain all possible different cases in one diagram (see Chapter 3). This difference can be seen by comparing Figure 2.13 and Figure 3.1.

For us, BPMN is primarily a medium of communication between developers (and even between developers and machines). There is no defined method to accompany this notation, though some practitioners try to fill this gap. For example, Jakob Freund and Bernd Rücker recommend in *Real-Life BPMN* that you start with a scenario-based approach that omits gateways (BPMN's way of modeling alternatives) [Freund/Rücker 2019]. Many practitioners slim down the extensive notation. Even if BPMN is used that way, we think that it is an approach aimed at expert modelers and that Domain Storytelling is a better way to have conversations between developers and domain experts.

How to Combine BPMN with Domain Storytelling

We have successfully used Domain Storytelling as the first step in implementing a semi-automated business process with a workflow engine. Domain Storytelling helps to design suitable TO-BE processes domain experts can agree on. Once the main scenarios have been identified and possible alternatives and error cases have been collected, the happy-path scenario is translated into formal BPMN. Piece by piece, the alternatives and error cases are integrated into the BPMN model.

Summary

In this chapter we showed you what else is in our toolbox besides Domain Storytelling. We are constantly expanding our toolbox and also keep finding new and useful ways of combining modeling approaches. We hope we could encourage you to try different modeling approaches out for yourself and figure out what works best for you.

We see Domain Storytelling as a member of the family of **collaborative modeling** methods. If you are interested in learning more about collaborative and visual modeling, you might want to look at the following:

- *Visual Collaboration Tools for Teams Building Software*—a book written by a community of practitioners (including us) [Baas-Schwegler/Rosa 2020].
- The *CoMoCamp*—a conference series dedicated to that topic [CoMoCamp Website].

With this we're coming to the end of Part I, in which we explained what Domain Storytelling is. Let's move on to Part II and see for which purposes it can be used.

Part II

<hr/>

Using and Adapting Domain Storytelling for Different Purposes

Part II of this book deals with the different problems and purposes Domain Storytelling can be used for. We will start by presenting a second, more comprehensive case study, and we will use that to discuss common problems and purposes, each in a separate chapter.

Even though we use the same case study in all the following chapters, you do not have to read them in order. Just start with Chapter 8 to learn about the case study and then pick the chapters that you are interested in.

Since Domain Storytelling is not bound to any particular approach to software development, we have tried to write the following chapters so that they work with all development methods. However, you will come across some terms that are well established in the *Domain-Driven Design*, *software architecture*, and *agile* communities.

In some situations, we have found it useful to combine Domain Storytelling with other modeling approaches. Therefore, we will give you some recommendations on how to combine methods to better achieve your goals.

That said, some prior knowledge of certain topics and methods will help you to get the most out of a chapter. If prior knowledge is recommended, we list it at the start of a chapter, but don't worry if you do not tick off all the items. You should still be able to understand our ideas.

Chapter 8

Case Study—Alphorn Auto Leasing Inc.

In Part I, "Domain Storytelling Explained," we have looked at the basics of Domain Storytelling with the help of a simple example that everybody recognizes from their daily lives: going to the movies at the Metropolis. Now we want to introduce and discuss topics that arise in more complex domains and show how Domain Storytelling can be used for real issues in actual projects. For this purpose, we will present a more complex example.

Alphorn Auto Leasing Inc. (Alphorn for short) is a car leasing company. Leasing a car from them means the customer is renting it for several years. Alphorn buys cars directly from manufacturers, leases them for a time period (most commonly for three years), and then sells the returned cars. Leasing is popular with companies because it's a way for them to offer company cars to their employees. Both employer and employees profit from tax incentives. Alphorn also leases cars to private customers. For them, leasing a car can be cheaper than buying a car with a bank loan.

Alphorn belongs to a group of stationary car dealerships. Alphorn's boss, Becky, has approved a new IT project that is vital for the company's future: They are going to build a new leasing software system that should be used both by the salespeople at the dealerships and by customers as an online service. Letting customers lease cars online will give Alphorn a competitive advantage. Becky assigns this important project directly to Harold, the head of IT. To get the project started, Harold hires two external consultants—us, Stefan and Henning.

Becky and Harold assemble a team of domain experts and IT staff who will work with us. The whole group is formed of the following:

- Becky, the boss
- Harold, head of IT

- Dave and Denise, developers
- Sandy, a salesperson
- Raymond, a risk manager
- Charley, a customer service agent

Explore Alphorn—The Domain as a Whole

As the first step in getting to know Alphorn, we invite salesperson Sandy and risk manager Raymond to a workshop. Ideally, we would have invited real customers too. Since this is difficult in our situation, we invite someone who can represent the customers' view: customer service agent Charley. In addition to the domain experts, the developers Denise and Dave are also on board because they will later have to write the software to support the new leasing processes.

We ask the domain experts to tell us a story that covers everything from the initial contact with a customer to returning the car after a three-year lease. Details are not important now; we just want to get an overview—a picture that will help us to discuss which activities should be supported by the new software and which are out of scope for the project.

Since the company leases cars to businesses and private customers, there are two potential stories to be told. We start with leasing to a private customer as this is the main target group for Alphorn's new online service.

Customer service agent Charley: "The whole thing starts with the customer choosing a car from the catalog."

Salesperson Sandy: "Yes, and after that they ask me for an offer."

Modeler Henning: "I'll draw that as sentences 1 and 2, starting at an actor 'customer.'"

Sandy: "When I've been asked, I offer a contract for that car and...."

After a lively modeling discussion of about three quarters of an hour, we end up with Alphorn 1 (see Figure 8.1).

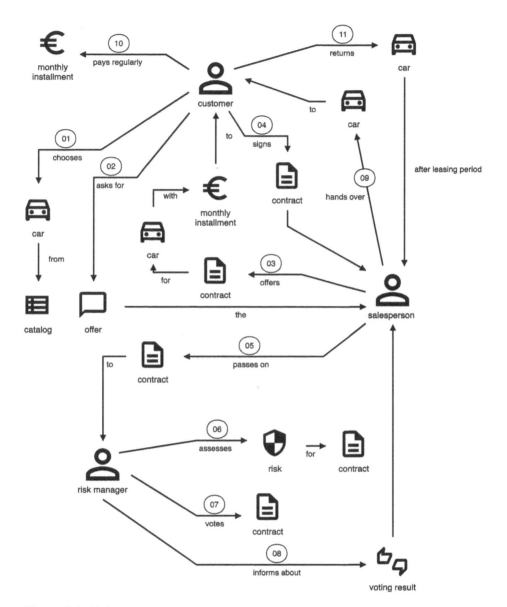

Figure 8.1 *Alphorn 1: Leasing a car—COARSE-GRAINED, PURE, AS-IS*

Sandy: "That pretty much describes what we are doing here at Alphorn."

Risk manager Raymond: "Currently, we risk managers get the signed contracts from the salespeople. That will probably change with the new system."

Drill Down into Risk Assessment—Understanding an Important Subdomain

After modeling how cars are leased to private customers in Alphorn 1 (see Figure 8.1) and to business customers (omitted here), we are ready to dig deeper into Alphorn's business. Risk assessment is one of the subdomains that will be affected by the project.

Passing on contracts from salespeople to risk managers makes no sense if customers are using the online service. Hence, we take a closer look at this subdomain and organize a second workshop. We invite not just Raymond but several other risk managers who have first-hand experience with business as well as private customers.

We look at all arrows that start or end at the actor "risk manager" in Alphorn 1 (see Figure 8.1) and ask the participants to tell us a story that begins with receiving a proposed contract and ends with passing on their voting result (sentences 5 to 8 in Alphorn 1). We agree on two assumptions. First, the story is about a contract for a private customer. Second, the story has a positive outcome—we want to understand the happy path first. Then, Raymond and his colleagues tell us the story shown in Figure 8.2, which we name Alphorn 2.

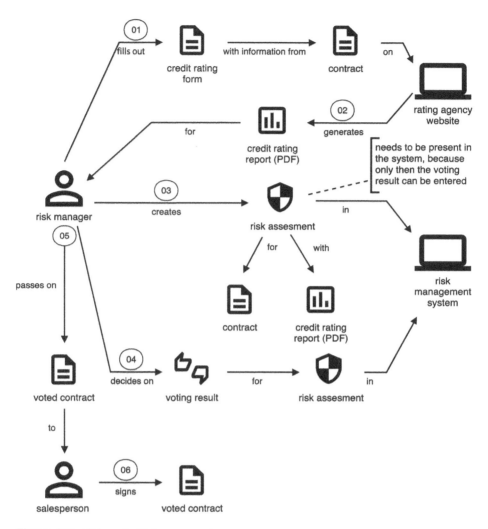

Figure 8.2 *Alphorn 2: Risk assessment—FINE-GRAINED, DIGITALIZED, AS-IS*

Clear Up Risk Assessment—Avoid Technical Jargon

Alphorn's risk assessment process seems a bit messy. We are unsure if we have collected enough knowledge to talk about potential requirements for the new online service. Some of the terms that the domain experts use sound very technical. We decide to ask Raymond and the other risk managers to tell the story again—but this time, they are to avoid all terminology that they have adopted from software systems. We ask them the following questions:

- "Imagine you were doing this without computers—how would you do it?"
- "What would that look like in a paper-based process?"
- "What would you call the things and information you work with?"

The resulting domain story is modeled as shown in Figure 8.3 and named Alphorn 3.

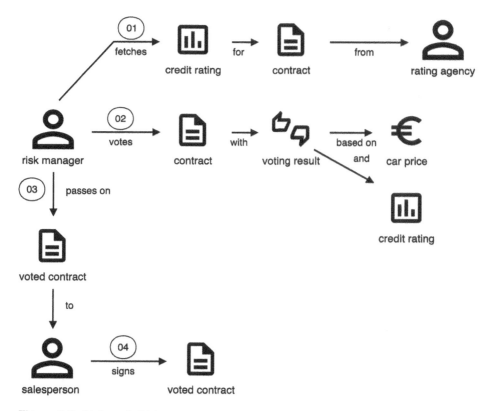

Figure 8.3 *Alphorn 3: Risk assessment—FINE-GRAINED, PURE, AS-IS*

Optimize Risk Assessment—The TO-BE Process

As soon as the pure process is on the wall, the domain experts start to discuss it. Raymond's boss, the head of the risk management department, says: "Having the salesperson sign the contract results in unnecessary work." There is clearly room for improving the existing processes. Together, we design a better TO-BE process—Alphorn 4 (see Figure 8.4). Now the risk manager signs the contract themselves instead of the salesperson.

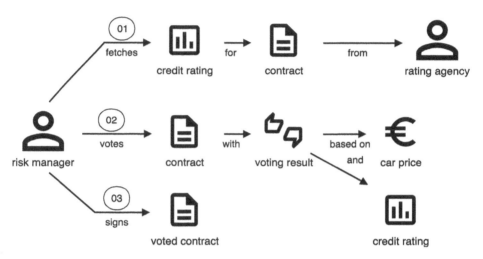

Figure 8.4 *Alphorn 4: Risk assessment—FINE-GRAINED, PURE, TO-BE*

Introduce New Software—Combine Business Processes with IT Support

After a couple of FINE-GRAINED domain stories about voting contracts, dealing with edge cases, and inconclusive credit ratings, we have a sound understanding of Alphorn's risk management. We still don't know all the details of the domain (like the algorithms for calculating resale values), but we can talk with Raymond and his colleagues about what they do.

Now, it's time to think about how their work will be affected by the new online service. We discuss how the online service should be integrated into the risk management process. One of the improvements we identified in Alphorn 4 (risk managers sign contracts) even makes its way into the DIGITALIZED process Alphorn 5 (see Figure 8.5).

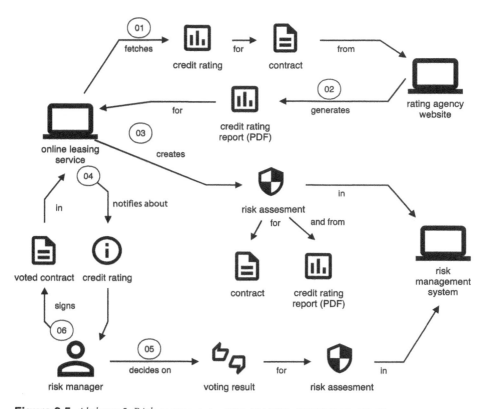

Figure 8.5 *Alphorn 5: Risk assessment*—FINE-GRAINED, DIGITALIZED, TO-BE

Summary

The Alphorn case study will accompany us throughout Part II. Table 8.1 provides an overview of the five domain stories that you have read so far.

Table 8.1 *Overview of the Alphorn Domain Stories*

Goal	Domain Story	Granularity	Point in Time	Domain Purity
Explore a new domain	Alphorn 1 (see Figure 8.1)	COARSE-GRAINED	AS-IS	PURE
Drill down into subdomains	Alphorn 2 (see Figure 8.2)	FINE-GRAINED	AS-IS	DIGITALIZED
Clear up a messy subdomain	Alphorn 3 (see Figure 8.3)	FINE-GRAINED	AS-IS	PURE
Optimize business processes	Alphorn 4 (see Figure 8.4)	FINE-GRAINED	TO-BE	PURE
Introduce new software	Alphorn 5 (see Figure 8.5)	FINE-GRAINED	TO-BE	DIGITALIZED

Over the course of several workshops, an icon set for Alphorn has emerged. Table 8.2 shows the complete icon set for reference.

Table 8.2 *The Icon Set for Alphorn Auto Leasing Inc.*

Icon	Building Block	Meaning
	Actor	A person
	Actor	A software system
	Work object	A document, form, or textual information
	Work object	A report, rating, or statistic
	Work object	A price, fee, installment, or other form of money
	Work object	A notification, event, or general information
	Work object	An actual car or information about a car
	Work object	Specifically used for a risk
	Work object	Specifically used for a voting result
	Work object	A date
	Work object	Specifically used for a catalog

After establishing the case study, we can now take a glance at the first purpose.

Chapter 9

Learning Domain Language

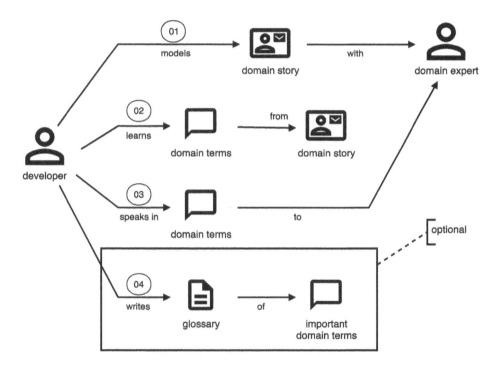

To build usable business software, you must first understand the domain. In this chapter, we will show how Domain Storytelling can help you to build up domain knowledge. Learning the language of the domain experts is the most important task because it is the key for effective conversations about business processes and software requirements.

This chapter is for you in the following cases:

- You are new to a domain (e.g., because you are a contractor) and need to "crunch" domain knowledge.

- You want to bring together domain experts from different departments to cross department boundaries and challenge assumptions.

- The software that you are working on does not use real terms from the domain, and you want to change that.

- You work in an organization where no real domain language exists, and you want one to emerge.

Stefan's Roadwork Story

A few years ago, two colleagues and I met with a public authority that plans roadwork for a large city. They had a simple question: How can software help us to better coordinate our construction sites?

To answer this question, we had to learn about a domain that we had no prior experience with. We needed to understand how the domain experts work, what they work with, and what problems they struggle with. We needed to be able to talk with the domain experts about the *problem space* to come up with ideas for the *solution space*.

Before our first workshop, we asked our client about their organization and which departments and roles were involved in planning roadwork. The number was surprisingly high, because it turned out that different departments were responsible for planning different types of streets. The same applied to bridges, tunnels, etc. To get to know every department and role involved, we scheduled three workshops, each three hours long. About seven domain experts from different departments participated in each workshop.

In those workshops, we asked the participants about their responsibilities. We collected their answers in a use case diagram that we projected on a wall. In one workshop, a domain expert complained: "Oh no, why do we have to model our business processes again?" He pointed at a shelf filled with folders. "Just look up what you need in our documentation!" But we had a feeling that the answers we were looking for were either not in the documentation or were buried so deep that we would struggle to find them. We assured the domain expert that we would take a look at the documentation later. After collecting some use cases and learning which ones were highly cooperative, we used Domain Storytelling to dive deeper into the domain. After a few sentences, even the skeptical domain expert realized that this was not an ordinary business process modeling workshop.

In a short time, we learned that a project manager for roadwork has dozens of factors to consider when planning their work. Every construction site must be planned in the context of all the other construction sites within a varying time frame and area. Over the course of the three workshops, we collected forty use cases and had the domain experts tell us five domain stories.

That body of acquired knowledge was sufficient for us to understand the problem space. In a fourth workshop, we presented our findings and asked, "Is that the problem you want us to solve?" The attending domain experts nodded in agreement.

The knowledge we gained from the five domain stories enabled us to talk with our client about their problem. Of course, we had to dive deeper into the domain to come up with solutions. During the workshops, the domain experts mentioned meetings and documents that play a role in coordinating roadwork. We asked for some examples and attended the meetings they mentioned. Quickly, ideas for designing the solution space came to our minds. We elaborated on these ideas with some more FINE-GRAINED domain stories and prototyping. Four months after the first workshop, we had a working software solution.

Speaking and Listening to Understand Each Other

Our experience in learning foreign languages is that you need to listen to other people speak that language. Repeat what you hear and pay attention to their feedback. Gradually, you will progress from individual words to phrases and to complete sentences. The more you speak, the faster you will learn.

With Domain Storytelling, you can employ the same principles when you are learning a new domain language. Let domain experts tell you a domain story. While you record the domain story, you repeat what you have heard. You ask about any terms you are not familiar with.

Unfortunately, it is easy for us humans to misunderstand one another. To prevent misunderstandings, visual modeling comes into play. The domain experts can hear *and* see whether you understand their story correctly. Having two feedback channels is better than having one. After just a few stories, you will be able to talk about the people, tasks, tools, work objects, and events in that domain.

Back to the Leasing Example

In the case study in Chapter 8, we explored the leasing domain with the COARSE-GRAINED domain story Alphorn 1 (see Figure 8.1). We learned nouns like "contract" and also verbs like "to sign." Then we moved on to FINE-GRAINED, PURE domain stories in the risk assessment subdomain. Many of the labels in these stories contain terms from the domain language. Let's revisit Alphorn 4 (see Figure 9.1). While modeling, look out for words that you don't understand. In sentence 1, for example, what exactly is a "credit rating"?

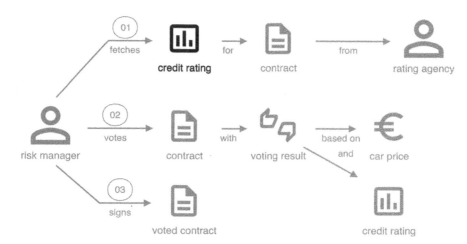

Figure 9.1 *Alphorn 4: Risk assessment—FINE-GRAINED, PURE, TO-BE*

Henning asks the domain expert for that subject matter—Raymond, the risk manager—for the meaning of these words. Stefan puts the answer in an annotation (see Figure 9.2).

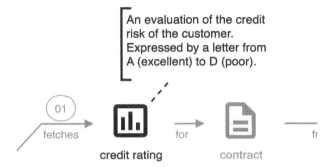

Figure 9.2 *Definition of a domain term*

To learn a domain language, it's best to focus on the PURE stories, because they are not tainted by the technical jargon that often comes with software systems. All levels of granularity can be interesting. To learn a language, you should begin with AS-IS domain stories. Later, when developing the language further, move on to TO-BE domain stories.

Domain stories are a good way to start learning a domain language. But they are usually not the only path you can follow to becoming fluent. In the next sections, we will briefly discuss techniques that complement Domain Storytelling.

Writing Glossaries

Writing a glossary is great for documenting what you have learned. But which terms should be included? Defining *all* terms from the domain is a tedious task, and many of those definitions will help nobody. Include only those terms that merit an explanation. With domain stories, it's easy to spot which terms should be part of the glossary: Typically, they have a defining annotation. But, of course, names of work objects, activities, and actors can be worth an entry as well.

Depending on the modeling tool, different methods exist for extracting the glossary from a domain story.

In an analog setting, big sticky notes are a good choice. Put the term as a heading in big letters on top and then write the definition below in smaller letters, like in Figure 9.3.

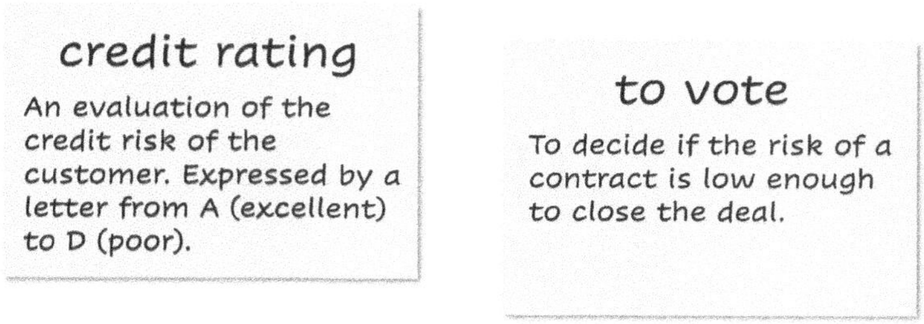

credit rating
An evaluation of the credit risk of the customer. Expressed by a letter from A (excellent) to D (poor).

to vote
To decide if the risk of a contract is low enough to close the deal.

Figure 9.3 *A glossary in sticky notes*

Put the stickies on a separated part of the wall or whiteboard. That way you can bring together the term definitions from several domain stories.

When using a digital tool, a simple spreadsheet file may be the right format. Table 9.1 with terms and definitions is the result.

Table 9.1 *Excerpt from the Risk Management Glossary*

Term	Definition
credit rating	An evaluation of the credit risk of the customer. Expressed by a letter from A (excellent) to D (poor).
to vote	To decide if the risk of a contract is low enough to close the deal.

Here again you can see that not only *nouns* are relevant. Understanding the *verbs* is equally important.

Maintaining a glossary can be cumbersome. We have worked with teams that kept their glossaries up-to-date by making them part of a user manual. Still, in many projects glossaries are not maintained and quickly become outdated. However, this is not necessarily a big problem. If writing the glossary helped you to learn the language, then it was worth the effort.

If you can refer to an existing glossary, then you can save some time. But do not confuse a glossary for a shortcut allowing you avoid having conversations with domain experts. After all, would you consider learning a foreign language just by reading a dictionary?

Observing How People Work

Observing how people work can be insightful for understanding a domain and thus complements Domain Storytelling. However, it would be hard to learn about a domain by just watching domain experts and not talking to them. Here is an analogy by Heinz Züllighoven:

Observing a Cook

Imagine you watch a cook who stirs a tomato sauce. You clock the time and measure that he stirs the sauce for exactly five minutes. Hence, you conclude that tomato sauce must always be stirred for five minutes. You repeat the process at home, but after five minutes of stirring, your sauce is still as watery as a tomato soup. Time was not the deciding factor. What you missed is that the cook stirred the sauce until it was of the right consistency.

There are more elaborate ethnographic methods than just silently observing domain experts. For example, you can do a *contextual inquiry* interview [Holtzblatt et al. 2005]. The interviewer observes the domain experts, but both also discuss the activities of the domain expert, and the interviewer shares their interpretations and insights.

Observation techniques help to discover unknown and implicit knowledge. You might notice things that the domain experts did not tell you at a Domain Storytelling workshop because it seemed too trivial or irrelevant to them. These techniques work best if you have at least some prior domain knowledge, because without context, it would be difficult to decide which activities you should observe. You would also have limited ability to interpret what you see.

Can't We Just Read the Docs?

How about skipping modeling and learning domain language from existing documentation instead? Unfortunately, good documentation is hard to find and even harder to write. We assume that's one of the reasons why the authors of the Agile Manifesto favor "Working software over comprehensive documentation" [Beck et al. 2001]. In some organizations, you will find process models, handbooks, guidelines, glossaries, specifications, regulations, and many other types of documents that contain domain language. In other organizations, you will find no documentation at all. At least then you don't have the hassle of determining which documents are relevant to you and if they are still valid and up-to-date.

It can be a challenge to choose between using existing documentation and starting from scratch. What has worked for us is to first learn some domain language with Domain Storytelling and then review existing documentation. That makes it much easier to decide what to read and what to do with the information you've found.

Organizations Speak Many Domain Languages

When you ask a heterogenous group of people to tell you a COARSE-GRAINED domain story, you will notice inconsistencies and generalizations. The reason for this is that the participants work in different subdomains. For example, Alphorn as a company is clearly in the "leasing" domain, and we already discovered a subdomain "risk assessment" (see Chapter 8, "Case Study—Alphorn Auto Leasing Inc."). This is a *core domain* of the company. That means it is at the heart of the business. Usually, you will find a rich and unique domain language within a core domain. But a leasing company also needs bookkeeping, marketing, and many other capabilities that can be considered domains in their own right. That means that the people you've invited speak different domain languages, although they all work for a leasing company.

> Organizations do not speak one unified, universal domain language!

In Stefan's roadwork story that opened this chapter, the domain experts came from core domains. All of them planned roadwork. Their "dialect" differed a little, because some plan roads and others bridges, but the whole workshop was about the parts of their job where they have to work together. We will give you another example from a different domain, but this time the subdomains use different languages:

Stefan's Browser Games Story

I moderated a Domain Storytelling workshop for a company that develops a marketplace for browser games. The company's service enables its customers to play games from several vendors, all with one account. In our first COARSE-GRAINED domain story, a new customer registered, put money into their account, and started to use one of the provided services.

> The domain experts could not agree on what an "account" is and which activities are associated with it. We altered the domain story several times, but there was always someone who objected. When I asked for details about the account, we found out that there were two separate accounts for each customer. One was tied to the customer (some called it the "customer account"), and one was associated with the games (known to some as the "gaming account"). From that point on, we used two separate work object icons for the two types of accounts. Therefore, the domain experts had to be explicit about which kind of account they were talking about.
>
> Later, distinguishing the two types of accounts was also crucial for inviting the right people to the follow-up workshops in which we wanted to model FINE-GRAINED domain stories.

In this anecdote, the term "account" turned out to have two different meanings, depending on the context (almost like a *homonym*). In one context, "account" refers to the billing and payment information of a customer. In another context, "account" means the behavior of the customer, e.g., which games they play. This is an important discovery! Uncovering such details will greatly improve your communication with the domain experts.

In addition to homonyms, you will also encounter *synonyms*—different words with the same meaning. Synonyms might originate from different subdomains.

Be careful: Even if you are so new to a domain that you need to understand things at a COARSE-GRAINED level, don't paint with too broad a stroke. Let the domain experts give you a concrete example. That will help you (and them!) to check if terms like "account," "client," "customer," "product," etc., are used with the same meaning or not.

Having different languages in different subdomains is natural. Attempts to wipe them out and replace them with a unified language generally prove to be unsuccessful (see Chapter 10, "Finding Boundaries"). You should *not* attempt to deal with differences in language by building abstractions or synthesizing an artificial language. Instead, use annotations to indicate synonyms and homonyms in your COARSE-GRAINED stories. To resolve differences in language, you need to dig into the subdomains with FINE-GRAINED AS-IS stories and work out an unambiguous language that is specific for the subdomain. In Domain-Driven Design, such a language is called a *ubiquitous language*.

Using Natural Languages

A domain language is based on natural languages like French, Arabic, Hindi, Nahuatl, etc. The examples we have used in this book are in English only, but we would like to show you that Domain Storytelling also works with other natural languages. Let's look at some everyday examples. We begin with an illustration in the authors' first language[1] in Figure 9.4.

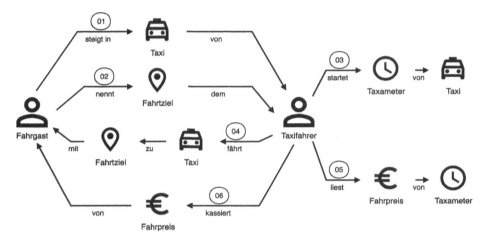

Figure 9.4 *In German: Traveling by taxi*

Written German is based on the Latin script (just like English, but with the ligature ß and umlauts—look at "ä" in sentence 4). Domain Storytelling also works with other scripts: Figure 9.5 uses the modern Persian (Farsi) script (which is based on the Arabic script and therefore written from right to left), and Figure 9.6 the Chinese script.[2]

Generally, you will use the natural language of the domain experts for modeling. In workshops that are comprised of people who speak different languages, there is usually a common language that can be used.

If an organization operates in several countries, there might even be several natural "business languages." We recommend you follow the idea of the ubiquitous language and avoid translations as long as possible. Sometimes an international team might request an exception. But beware: many words cannot be translated without loss of information, shift in meaning, or at all.

---

1. Stefan was born in Austria and Henning in Germany.
2. We thank Samaneh Javanbakht and Isabella Tran for translation and transcription.

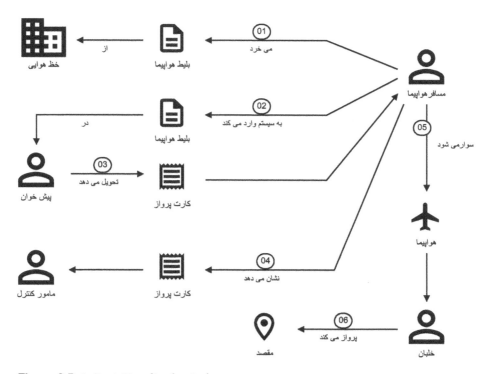

Figure 9.5 *In Farsi: Traveling by airplane*

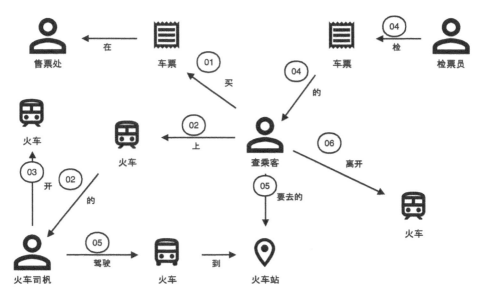

Figure 9.6 *In Chinese: Traveling by train*

Lost in Translation

Many organizations employ *business analysts* or *requirements engineers* who serve as intermediaries between domain experts and developers. These roles are often interpreted as professional "translators" who take input from domain experts and translate it to requirements that development teams can implement. Sometimes, even Scrum's *product owner* [Rubin 2013] is implemented as a "translating" role rather than an "owning" role.

Good translators are hard to find. They carry a lot of responsibility. Nuance gets easily lost in translation. Translators might make assumptions and communicate them as facts, or they might not have the technical background required to ask the right questions for software development.

However, many business analysts and requirements engineers have skills that domain experts sometimes lack—like being able to articulate what is expected from a piece of software or finding the right level of abstraction. Also, many developers would not be able to get the right information from domain experts on their own.

We do not advise to have intermediaries work as translators because developers might be led to believe there is no more need for them to learn the domain language. Rather, it makes sense to use the skill set of business analysts and requirements engineers to bridge the gap between business and IT through moderation and facilitation. They should help domain experts and developers to communicate with each other.

> Moderators can help the development team to become fluent in domain language.

Therefore, we suggest to add the role of a moderator to your cross-functional development team. This role can be assumed by anyone in the team who has the necessary skills. A business analyst or requirements engineer would be a good fit for that role, allowing them to integrate into the development team. The moderator's goal is to help the development team become fluent in domain language. They do so by facilitating and teaching collaborative modeling with methods such as Domain Storytelling.

What to Read Next?

Differences in language are a good way to learn about the boundaries that exist within an organization. The contexts that are defined by different domain languages tell you more about the structure of an organization than org charts and the scope of existing software systems. Hence, domain languages can be used as a guide to split up monolithic software systems or to find a good scope for new software. This will be covered in Chapter 10, "Finding Boundaries."

Once you are able to speak a domain language, you can talk about requirements more effectively. We will show you more ways Domain Storytelling can help you with requirements elicitation in Chapter 11, "Working with Requirements."

The language becomes ubiquitous through being used in the source code. Which domain terms to use as names for classes, methods, functions, and variables is the topic of Chapter 12, "Modeling in Code."

Finally, there are other collaborative modeling techniques that are helpful for learning a language (see Chapter 7, "Relationship to Other Modeling Methods"). Combining methods can sometimes be useful too. For instance, *Example Mapping* is a good follow-up to Domain Storytelling.

Chapter 10

Finding Boundaries

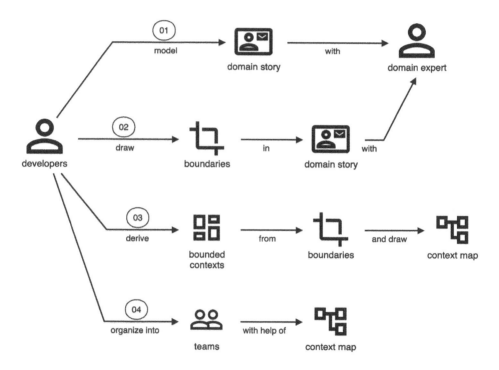

Many domains are too big to be understood and modeled as a whole. In such cases, you need to break down a domain into manageable units. In this chapter, we elaborate an important step in this process: finding the boundaries between subdomains.

This chapter is for you in the following cases:

- You are struggling with a monolith and want to re-organize it or split it into more manageable parts.

- You want to design microservices or self-contained systems.

- You want to apply Domain-Driven Design (DDD) and have difficulties identifying bounded contexts.

- Your development team has become too big to work efficiently, and you want to split it into several teams.

- You already have more than one development team and want to find out how you can organize the work for these teams.

In this chapter, we will come across some software development terms and concepts that we will explain only briefly. For more details, please see the references provided. In particular, we will refer to the following:

- Strategic DDD vocabulary like *subdomain*, *bounded context*, and *context map* [Vernon 2016]

- Architecture styles (*monolithic*, *modular* [Lilienthal 2019], *microservices* [Newman 2015], and *self-contained systems* [SCS Website])

- Principles for organizing development teams, such as *cross-functional teams* [Rubin 2013] and *Conway's Law* [Conway 1968]

Henning's Aircraft Maintenance Story

A big airline reached out and asked me to structure a large system for the technical maintenance of their aircraft. A child's dream came true for me when the IT manager gave me a tour of the hangars and showed me how the mechanics worked on the planes. There were small ones and big ones; as a highlight, we climbed into a 747 to take a glance at all the different technology that is built into a modern airplane.

Back in the office, we met with a group of 20 people. We started by modeling the most important business processes of aircraft maintenance. We drew COARSE-GRAINED, PURE domain stories. This overview proved useful for getting everyone on the same page and finding out what we still had to do.

The domain experts told me that the sentences in these stories could be considered business processes in their own right. In fact, most of the work objects appeared only once per domain story. To me, each of these (apparently cloud-level) sentences felt a bit like an item on a checklist rather than sentences that build on each other to create a compelling story. I suspected that each sentence would be its own context, probably even more than one context.

We had to narrow the scope to identify useful boundaries in the domain, so we scheduled a series of follow-up workshops. Each had 5–8 participants who were experts in the respective area.

In the follow-up workshops, we dove deeper into the domain while still modeling COARSE-GRAINED, now at kite level. In the emerging stories, we found groups of coherent activities. These groups quickly developed further into 20 candidates for bounded contexts.

The context map that we distilled from the domain stories later became the basis for the team organization and new architecture of the system.

The Joy of Multiple Models

A single conceptual model is a tricky beast to work with.
—Martin Fowler [Fowler 2003b]

One of the challenges in building software is to structure it in a way that is comprehensible for developers. If a domain is too big to be understood as a whole, then it is too big to be modeled in software as a whole. A better solution is to have multiple models that cover self-contained parts of a domain instead. This enables the software and the development team to grow.

As we write this book, splitting monoliths is one of the hottest topics in software development. It is also one of the biggest problems that some of our clients experience. We have seen many large (> 1,000,000 LOC) legacy systems that had an adequate technical architecture and were nevertheless considered a *big ball of mud* [Foote/Yoder 1997] by their developers.

Many of these barely comprehensible software systems are the result of a fundamental misunderstanding: That software should be based on a single, common model of the domain. And that this model is unambiguous. And that it should contain all properties of the real world in as much detail as possible.

DDD uses the term *domain model*, but it does not mean a company-wide model. If an entire organization is described with just one model, every software requirement needs to be understood in the context of this one model. The problem with this approach is that the model grows bigger and bigger. It tends to become a tangled mess that cannot be understood as a whole. A *big ball of mud* model leads to *big ball of mud* software.

DDD recognizes that, in real life, there is more than one truth, and a company needs several domain models. Take a look at central domain concepts in your organization, e.g., "account," "client," "customer," or "product." People will use the same term with different meanings in different parts of a domain—the so-called subdomains each have their own domain model.

 "The one" model as the source of pure and unambiguous truth is an illusion.

A Heuristic for Finding Subdomains

A good understanding of subdomains will help you identify technical boundaries in the form of microservices [Newman 2015], self-contained systems [SCS Website], or modules within a monolith (also called a *modular monolith* or *modulith* by some).

We found that domain stories can help with defining the boundaries within a domain: You can use domain stories to find out which activities—from a domain expert's perspective—belong together. Thus, the domain can be broken down into subdomains. We consider this a heuristic rather than a strict rule.

 Subdomains consist of activities that belong together from an **actor's perspective**.

Applying the Heuristic

This "recipe" describes our heuristic:

1. Find meaningful scenarios that cover the essentials of the domain.

2. Model those scenarios as domain stories. The scope should be COARSE-GRAINED, AS-IS, and PURE (see Chapter 4, "Scope"). Coarse granularity is cloud or kite level. PURE stories work best, because they are about activities that are not tainted by current software systems. You probably want to remove the impact of the existing systems on the organization and start thinking about subdomains completely from scratch.

3. Within the domain story (or stories), find activities that belong together. (To help you with finding cohesive activities, we have compiled some indicators in the next section.)

4. Cluster the activities into groups to make the subdomain boundaries visible. Since actors may act in more than one subdomain, place them outside the groups to make it clear that the actors are not considered part of the subdomain.

We will apply this recipe to Alphorn now.

Back to the Leasing Example

We have already taken steps 1 and 2 together with salesperson Sandy, risk manager Raymond, and customer service agent Charley in Chapter 8, "Case Study—Alphorn Auto Leasing Inc." Together with them, we modeled a happy-path scenario as COARSE-GRAINED domain story Alphorn 1 (reprinted in Figure 10.1).

Let's now take the other steps.

When we ask the domain experts which activities belong together, Sandy the salesperson says, "Sentences 1 to 5, that is the 'offering' part of the story. Once I have passed the contract on to the risk manager, it is literary out of my hands." We group those activities together and name them accordingly (see Figure 10.2).

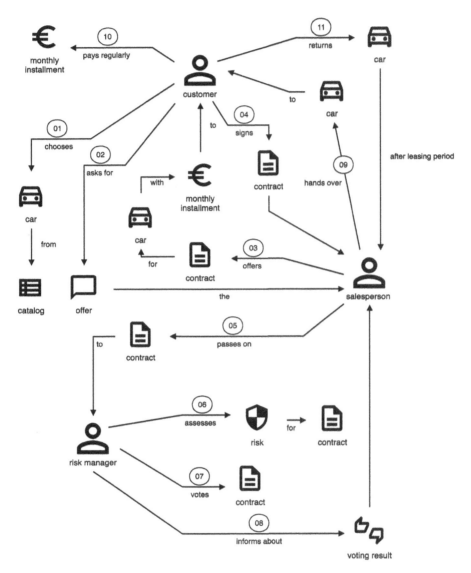

Figure 10.1 *Alphorn 1: Leasing a car—COARSE-GRAINED, PURE, AS-IS*

Next, we ask Raymond if the risk managers' part of the story should be grouped in one or in several sets of activities. He answers that sentences 6 to 8 belong together. Every contract has to be processed in this way. We agree on a name for this group of activities—"risk assessment" (see Figure 10.3).

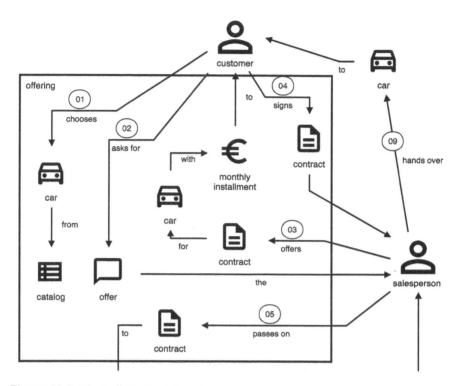

Figure 10.2 *The "offering" subdomain*

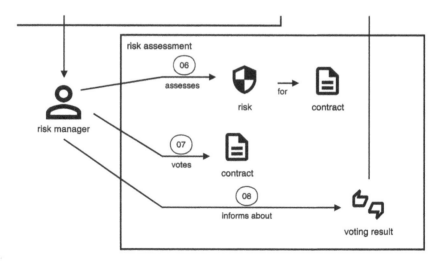

Figure 10.3 *The "risk assessment" subdomain*

We continue the discussion with the domain experts until we have reached the result shown in Figure 10.4. Since this is a further iteration of domain story Alphorn 1 (see Figure 10.1), we name it Alphorn 1a.

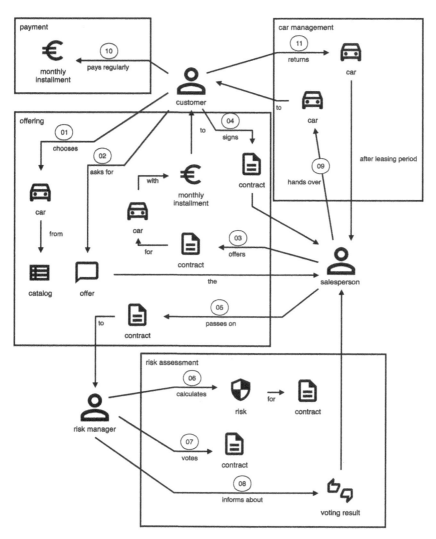

Figure 10.4 *Alphorn 1a: Leasing a car—*COARSE-GRAINED, PURE, AS-IS—*grouped by subdomain*

In summary, we have derived four subdomains from a COARSE-GRAINED domain story. That domain story describes just one scenario. If we look at more scenarios, most of these subdomains will appear again. Also, we will probably find other subdomains.

We also noticed that the offering subdomain is quite large. In our experience, this suggests that we will encounter inconsistent language as we continue to analyze the subdomain. In this case, we would further split the subdomain.

Sometimes, it is not so easy to figure out where one subdomain ends and another one begins, or if a subdomain should be split into smaller ones. In such cases, we recommend you model domain stories that play *within* one subdomain. Check how well those stories fit within the boundaries that you have proposed. Test the subdomain boundaries by looking for signs that the domain story reaches into other subdomains. Refine the boundaries and consider other heuristics as well (see the following section).

Indicators for Subdomain Boundaries

Indicators are not definitive proof that there is a boundary. They just provide some clues about what to look for. We have collected some indicators we have come across repeatedly. This list is not exhaustive, but we think it is helpful:

- **Actor produces result on their own:** An actor completes several related activities independently, producing a meaningful outcome. Often, the actor then passes the result on to other actors. An example is "risk assessment," as shown in Figure 10.4.

- **One-way information flow:** A handover between actors—an actor *A* transfers a work object to actor *B*, and there is no information flowing back to actor *A* (neither directly nor indirectly). This means that *A* is not involved in whatever *B* does with the transferred work object.

- **Different triggers:** Customer service agent Charley has told us that the customer's inquiry triggers the offering—an example of a request-based trigger. Once the car has been handed over, the customer must pay the monthly installment—an example of a time-based trigger (see Figure 10.5).

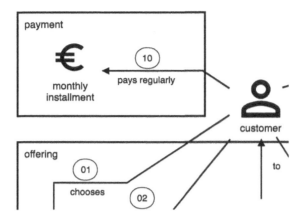

Figure 10.5 *Indicator: Different triggers—here: time-based*

- **Activities supporting something that is not in the picture:** In another domain story, Raymond tells us that creating a "risk report" is one of the risk managers' activities. However, this risk report is not used by other actors in the story. Since the report was created for a reason, it will probably be used in another subdomain that is not relevant for this domain story.

- **Differences in language:** The same work object is given different names by different actors. Or the same name is used with a (slightly) different meaning. (The second case is much harder to spot.)

- **Different use of the same thing:** The same work object is used for significantly different tasks. For example, at Alphorn, the contract is "signed" by the customer and "voted" by risk managers. Signing is a legal act that creates a relationship. Voting takes place in a financial context—it is done to mitigate the financial risk for Alphorn.

From Subdomains to Bounded Contexts

So far, we have analyzed the *problem space*, where subdomains exist. If your goal is to build software, you have to transition from the problem space into the *solution space*. In DDD, this means designing *bounded contexts*. A bounded context implements an unambiguous domain model with a ubiquitous language. If a subdomain and a bounded context have a 1:1 relationship, you can think of them as two sides of the same coin.

Defining bounded contexts is a design process. DDD expert Nick Tune distinguishes five main categories of criteria for designing boundaries [Tune 2019a]:

- **Business value:** Design decisions aligned to the business strategy

- **Domain:** Design decisions aligning boundaries with the problem domain

- **Sociopolitical:** Design decisions driven by the needs of the people building the systems

- **Technical:** Design decisions affected by the technical requirements of a system (e.g., performance, security)

- **User experience:** Design decisions that have an impact on how users experience the system

As you can see, alignment with (sub)domains is one of several criteria for finding bounded contexts. Often, there is no single, obvious solution. Trade-offs need to be considered. For that reason, the DDD community has resorted to the use of heuristics for finding bounded contexts.

Heuristics for Finding Bounded Contexts

Several DDD practitioners have shared their experience:

- *DDD Heuristics* was initiated by Rebecca Wirfs-Brock and Kenny Baas-Schwegler. The webpage collects heuristics that are relevant for DDD, including some for bounded contexts [DDDHeuristics Website].

- Nick Tune's *Tech Strategy Blog* [Tune Blog].

- The DDD Crew Repository contains useful tools [DDDCrew Website].

- In addition to other DDD topics, Mathias Verraes writes about boundary finding in his blog [Verraes Blog].

Bounded context is one of the most important concepts of Domain-Driven Design. In the DDD literature,[1] you will find methods that help with reasoning about bounded contexts. One useful tool is a *context map* that shows how bounded contexts are connected. The context map shows a combined view of what can be learned by modeling several stories. Creating a context map is the logical next step after defining bounded contexts. Let's look at a first version of an Alphorn context map in Figure 10.6. It includes the four bounded contexts that we had identified so far and one relationship between offering and risk assessment.

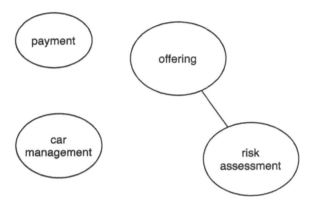

Figure 10.6 *Beginning of a context map for Alphorn*

This is just the beginning of *context mapping*. The next step is to describe the relationships and interfaces. We are not going into that here, because it is covered in the DDD literature.

Bounded contexts are necessary to enable independent teams and keep software changeable. But business processes usually need integration. This requires a behavioral view of business processes. Domain Storytelling supports this shared view by bringing together people from different subdomains so that they can tell us what happens when a business process crosses from one subdomain to the next.

Domain stories provide a behavioral view that complements the structural view of a context map and the temporal view of EventStorming. That means that Domain Storytelling is not only a means for finding bounded contexts; it is also a means for visualizing collaboration across context boundaries.

---

1. See for example Vaughn Vernon's *Implementing Domain-Driven Design* [Vernon 2013] and Michael Plöd's *Domain-Driven Design by Example* [Plöd 2020].

Context boundaries should separate models, not people.

From Context Boundaries to Team Boundaries

Once we have defined the context boundaries, we can use this knowledge to find the team boundaries. With a large software system (like the monolithic big ball of mud we described earlier), there are many people working, usually more than fit into one team. It makes sense to divide them into several teams and ask the question, who does what? If you have more than one team, it is generally a good idea to not let different teams work on the same parts of the system.

Collective code ownership [Beck 2000] is desirable inside a team, but not across team boundaries.

A classical approach to development team organization is to split the teams by the architectural layer. One UI team, one business logic team, one database team. This is a horizontal cut. Because of Conway's Law,[2] the agile community (and we as part of it) think this is a bad idea. A more modern idea is to have cross-functional teams. This would mean a vertical cut. But where do we draw the boundaries between teams? That is where bounded contexts come into play.

One rule of design is that one bounded context should belong exclusively to one team. The reason is that we don't want several teams to work on the same part of the software, so they do not destroy each other's work. On the other hand, this does not mean that one team can have only one bounded context.

So, when dividing your developers into several teams, make sure that every team has at least one bounded context. When we apply this rule to Alphorn, where we have three development teams, one possible split would be as depicted in Figure 10.7.

The assignment of bounded contexts to teams may change over time. One possibility is to start with one team that takes care of all the bounded contexts. If the team grows, eventually a point will be reached where it is has to be split into two teams. At this point, assign the contexts to the resulting teams.

---

2. Conway's Law basically says that the architecture of the software will have the same structure as the organization of the teams that build it [Conway 1968].

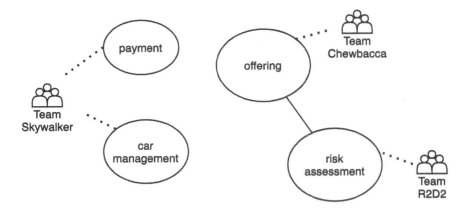

Figure 10.7 *Team organization at Alphorn*

What to Read Next?

Finding boundaries is hard. In fact, it is probably the toughest challenge we write about in this book. Reasoning about subdomains and bounded contexts with Domain Storytelling is just one of many useful tools. We recommend that you check out the references provided in this chapter.

You can also try big-picture EventStorming and look for *boundary events*—for example, events that indicate a handover, a changed state, or a point of no return. Alberto Brandolini calls those events *pivotal*, and what they separate *business phases*. For more information, read his article "Discovering Bounded Contexts with EventStorming" [Brandolini 2020]. Nick Tune came up with a workshop recipe that makes use of EventStorming, a *bounded context design canvas* [Tune 2019b], and an adaptation of Domain Storytelling that he calls *Domain Message Flow Modelling* [Tune 2021].

If you are satisfied with the boundaries that you have found, one of the next questions to ask for every bounded context is this: Do we build this part of the software ourselves ("make"), or do we buy an off-the-shelf solution ("buy")?

- If the decision is "make," Chapter 12, "Modeling in Code," describes how to implement the domain model.

- If the decision is "buy," read Chapter 14, "Deciding Make or Buy and Choosing Off-the-Shelf Software," to decide which of the standard products is the right one for you.

Once you decide to dig deeper, consider learning more about the language (see Chapter 9) that is spoken within each subdomain (called *ubiquitous language* in DDD).

When you have organized your teams, the next thing to do is to define what the teams should do (e.g., with agile *user stories*, see *User Stories Applied* [Cohn 2004]) and to organize that work (e.g., in a *product backlog*, see *Essential Scrum* [Rubin 2013]). How that is done is the topic of Chapter 11, "Working with Requirements."

Chapter 11

Working with Requirements

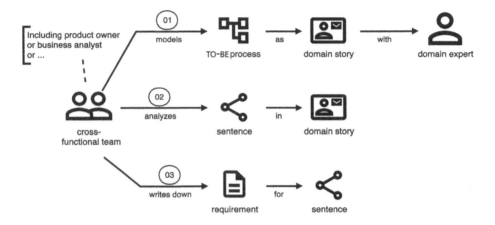

In the preceding chapters, we discussed how to understand a domain and its language. We showed you how to find team and context boundaries. Sometimes, this is all that development teams need to jump directly into code. However, usually jumping from scenarios to code is a bit too challenging, and you need to bridge the gap between domain knowledge and requirements. We will show you how to derive requirements from domain stories so that you can discuss priorities and viable products.

This chapter is for you in the following cases:

- You consider yourself one of the following:
  - Product owner
  - Product manager
  - Business analyst
  - Requirements engineer
  - Developer in a cross-functional team that does its own requirements analysis

- You want to do any of the following:
  - Find out what the software you build should actually do
  - Add context to requirements

- You work with either of the following:
  - User stories
  - Product backlogs

In this chapter, we will come across some software development terms and concepts that we will explain only briefly. For more details, please see the references provided. In particular, we will refer to these terms:

- Agile/Scrum terminology: *user story* [Cohn 2004], *product owner, sprint, product backlog* [Rubin 2013]
- User Story Mapping [Patton 2014]
- Use cases [Cockburn 2001]

Stefan's Call for Tenders Story

If a public institution in the European Union needs software, it can't simply hire any company. It is obliged by law to call for tenders. That means the institution must write a requirements document. Companies can then submit a tender for the contract. Finally, one of the contenders is selected based on price, qualifications, and the proposed solution.

Some time ago, our company won such a tender. The requirements specification document amounted to 300 pages, describing (among many other things) 80 use cases. Personally, I am not a big fan of these kinds of documents. Since I have written one or two myself, I know that no matter how much skill and time go into them, they are always outdated, incomplete, and—to put it simply—wrong. Nevertheless, those 80 use cases were among the best I had ever read: They contained a main success scenario, variation scenarios, preconditions, primary actors, goals, triggers, and a lot of other useful information.

Our customer's business analyst had done a great job, but as soon as we started working on the software, my colleagues and I realized that the use cases were not sufficient to really understand the domain. We did not know enough about the business processes and the context of the requirements.

At the kick-off workshop, I decided to pull Domain Storytelling out of my toolbox. I did this because the business process that we wanted to analyze was highly cooperative, involving multiple actors and systems. The customer's team included the business analyst and about five domain experts who would later use our software. Together with two of my colleagues, I modeled three happy-path scenarios as MEDIUM-GRAINED, DIGITALIZED, AS-IS, domain stories. We were able to gain a better understanding of the domain. In particular, we understood the shortcomings of the existing solution, which motivated several of the requirements.

When we all met again about a month later, we were interested in the solution space. In a second round of Domain Storytelling, we used the same three happy-path scenarios as we did the first time, except that now we had the domain experts tell us about the TO-BE processes. Now, we got to understand the interplay of the use cases.

Another three months and several implemented use cases later, we had reached a point where we had to think about going live with the first release. Our customer had planned an incremental rollout—some users would switch to our new software, and others would continue to use the old software. To make that possible, we had to enable collaboration between the two software systems. We needed to design a collaborative, software-supported workflow, and again we chose Domain Storytelling for that purpose. This time, the scope was FINE-GRAINED, DIGITALIZED, and TO-BE. During the workshop, we realized that the newly designed, software-supported workflow was not backed by the requirements document. However, it was easy to derive new requirements from the domain story. Basically, we just had to transcribe the activities into text form.

Besides domain stories, we also used mock-ups and walk-throughs of implemented functionality.

By the way, our team grew by approximately one developer per month. Retelling the domain stories helped the new team members understand the domain. So, it became part of the team's onboarding process. But that's another story.

Software Development as a Series of Conversations

Building software does not mean a programmer sits alone in a dark room typing code into a computer. Instead, it is highly interactive and communicative. Over the whole life cycle of a software system, developers, domain experts, and other stakeholders talk to each other again and again. Of course, it involves typing code into a computer (though usually not alone and not in the dark), but this is only one part of the process, and it alternates with conversations. Coding is a conversation too: with the computer, with other developers (in the form of *pair programming* [Beck 2000] or *mob programming* [Zuill 2014]), and even with the developers who have to read the code in the future.

This series of conversations will make it clearer and clearer what is required from a system. We believe that working with requirements is not an objective, strictly analytical process. Descriptions of requirements such as text or diagrams are never "complete" or objectively "right." Rather, we see them as something that the stakeholders involved create from their own perspective. As Christiane Floyd observes:

> We do not analyze requirements; we construct them from our own perspective. This perspective is affected by our personal priorities and values, by the methods we use as orientation aids, and by our interaction with others. [Floyd 1992]

For that to work, the stakeholders must align their perspectives, priorities, and values, at least to an extent that allows teams to produce artifacts. These artifacts—running software, mock-ups, paper prototypes, etc.—can be evaluated by the stakeholders, thus continuing the conversation. Different modeling methods are useful at several stages in this continued conversation, with Domain Storytelling being just one of them. The rest of this chapter illustrates how you can facilitate a conversation about requirements with the help of Domain Storytelling, user stories, and User Story Mapping.

Revisiting the Metaphor for Granularity

In Chapter 4, "Scope," we used Alistair Cockburn's "goal levels" metaphor to describe the granularity of domain stories (see Figure 11.1). Cockburn originally developed this metaphor for use cases—a description format for requirements. In this chapter, we will use the metaphor for both domain stories *and* requirements. We think it fits in wonderfully with the idea of software development as a series of conversations. The different levels help to steer the discussion in the right direction.

Cloud Level

Kite Level

Sea Level

Fish Level

Clam Level

Figure 11.1 *Different goal levels*

From Domain Stories to Requirements

Domain stories are a great medium for moving from a spoken conversation to a written requirement that is just formal enough to be planned, estimated (if you are into estimations), and implemented. However, we do not propose a strict top-down process of decomposing high-level requirements into low-level requirements. We think that such a "waterfall" approach would not work in the real world. A conversation about requirements may start COARSE-GRAINED and evolve to FINE-GRAINED, but it is not a one-way street. For us, software development is not a process in which first the requirements are defined and then the software is programmed, but a constant cycle of discussing the requirements and their constructive implementation.

In the following sections, we will present a step-by-step "recipe" to break down domain stories, mixing up different "ingredients." Finally, we will apply the recipe to the Alphorn example.

A Recipe for Breaking Down a Domain Story

For our recipe we need some ingredients:

- A method for finding functional requirements: Domain Storytelling
- A method for writing requirements down: user stories
- A method for organizing requirements: User Story Mapping

We assume that one team works on supporting a business process within a bounded context. Further, we assume that the team has access to domain experts. Now you're ready to begin.

1. The team models the business process as a MEDIUM-GRAINED TO FINE-GRAINED domain story, starting with the most important scenario (usually, the happy path). PURE and DIGITALIZED TO-BE stories both work.

2. For every activity in the story, ask if it should be supported by the new software system. As a general rule of thumb, if an activity should be supported by IT, write a kite-level requirement for it. These requirements will become the backbone of your backlog.

3. Model alternative scenarios and, if necessary, more FINE-GRAINED domain stories. Collect information about exceptions, possible errors, edge cases, and so on as annotations.

4. Walk through the new domain stories and the annotations. Again, for every new sentence, write one requirement on kite level or sea level. Check your annotations—see which ones should become a requirement and write them down as well.

5. Organize the requirements by mapping the FINE-GRAINED requirements to the backbone, creating a user story map.

The team now has a structured backlog of kite- and sea-level requirements. The backlog will neither be complete nor are all the requirements ready for implementation. However, the team will have a sound understanding of the functional requirements and how they add up to a workable business process.

Next, we will look at the method for writing requirements down with user stories (steps 2 and 4 in the recipe) and the method for organizing requirements with User Story Mapping (step 5).

Writing Down Requirements as User Stories

Spoken conversations are vital to discovering requirements. Sooner or later, you will need a memory aid. Domain stories are a helpful tool, just like other diagrams, mock-ups, etc., but often a short text is the most expressive way to capture a conversation. There are many ways of writing such a text. Currently the most popular format is the *user story*.

Caution: *user story* sounds similar to *domain story*, but they are different things. It's a bit like *Java* and *JavaScript*.

Please keep in mind that user stories are first and foremost oral conversations. To preserve the essence of such a conversation, people have followed simple templates, such as this one:

As a < type of user >, I want < some goal > so that < some reason >.[1]

This schema is like a little checklist for the conversation. It also matches the structure of a sentence in a domain story:

As an < actor > I want to < activity plus work object > so that …

So, *actor* becomes *type of user*, and *activity* plus *work object* describes the *goal*. And where do we get *some reason* from? This "why" can sometimes be found in the annotations. Sometimes it is not directly in the domain story but comes from the conversations.

A user story should not be confused with a specification just because it can take written form. We cannot stress enough that a user story is a "promise for a conversation" [Cockburn Origin], meaning that the written text is a by-product and not a substitute for communication. This aspect is often neglected in practice and is one of the reasons that user stories are sometimes viewed critically.

Building a Backlog of Requirements with User Story Mapping

We already introduced User Story Mapping [Patton 2014] in Chapter 7, "Relationship to Other Modeling Methods." There, we briefly described how User Story

---

1. There are many different templates for user stories; we chose a template popularized by Mike Cohn [Cohn 2004].

Mapping guides you through a conversation about requirements. For us, Domain Storytelling plays this guiding role. However, we use User Story Mapping as a planning instrument for cross-functional, agile teams to do the following:

- Talk to a product owner about priorities and increments

- Clarify which requirements need to be worked out in detail next

- Never lose sight of the context of a user story

In the context of our "recipe," we apply User Story Mapping as an additional "ingredient" after domain stories have been created. Typically, we start the User Story Mapping workshop by unrolling the sentences of a MEDIUM-GRAINED domain story (or stories) into what User Story Mapping calls the *backbone*: a series of user stories (about kite level), arranged in a timeline from left to right. This is the horizontal dimension of the user story map. It represents a business process or a user journey.

When the backbone is finished, it is time to move on into the vertical dimension, which is used to detail requirements and prioritize them. The high-level user stories are elaborated and refined through detailed user stories (sea level to fish level). MEDIUM- and FINE-GRAINED domain stories will help here. With the resulting user story map/product backlog, the product owner and team are ready to plan the next sprint.

Back to the Leasing Example

Let's apply the recipe from earlier to Alphorn. We start with the team that builds the bounded context "offering." For that purpose, we meet with developers Dave and Denise, and with Sandy, who represents the sales team (the experts for this context). They look at domain story Alphorn 1a from Chapter 10, "Finding Boundaries," again. They decide that their part in this story (see Figure 11.2) contains enough detail for deriving the backbone, so this serves as step 1 of the recipe (modeling a MEDIUM-GRAINED TO-BE domain story). They go on to step 2—creating the backbone.

The first sentence in Figure 11.2, "Customer chooses car from catalog," is an activity that should be supported by the software system and thus becomes a kite-level requirement: "choose car." We write it on a sticky note (see Figure 11.3).

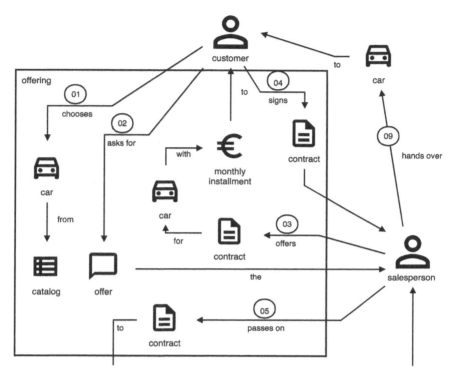

Figure 11.2 *The bounded context "offering" from Alphorn 1a*

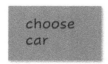

Figure 11.3 *A kite-level requirement for our user story map*

We leave out "from catalog" for now, because it describes one of several ways of achieving this goal. "Choose a car from catalog" is already a sea-level requirement, so we write it down but put it aside until we arrive at step 4 of the recipe.

The workshop participants move on sentence by sentence. The team decides that the second sentence, "Customer asks for offer," and the third sentence, "Salesperson offers contract for car," can be condensed into one kite-level requirement: "offer contract." The customer will still need to sign the contract (sentence four). Finally, the contract needs to be passed on for risk assessment. A backbone emerges, visualized as a horizontal sequence of sticky notes (see Figure 11.4).

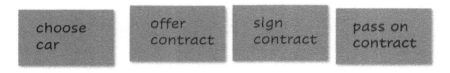

Figure 11.4 *Backbone of kite-level requirements*

The team tries to develop the user story map further by modeling FINE-GRAINED domain stories for their bounded context. As always, we let our domain expert (in this case Sandy) tell their story. Denise takes the lead in modeling and discussion:

Developer Denise: "You offer a contract with a monthly installment, and the customer signs the contract. Can you please tell us what you are doing in more detail?"

Salesperson Sandy: "Last time, we started with what you called the 'happy path.' Do you want me to go back to the best-case scenario?"

Denise: "Yes, please."

Sandy: "First, I take a contract form with a new contract number. I fill out the contract with the details of the car and its price."

Denise: "I will model this as your first activity: 'Salesperson fills out contract.'"

Sandy: "Now I am ready to calculate the monthly installment for the contract. I calculate it from price, term, and interest."

Denise: "Step 2: 'Salesperson calculates installment.'"

Sandy: "Finally, I offer the contract with all details to the customer. If they agree with it, they sign it."

Denise: "I will model this as two steps—step 3 is 'Salesperson offers contract,' and step 4 is 'Customer signs contract.'"

This conversation results in the domain story shown in Figure 11.5.

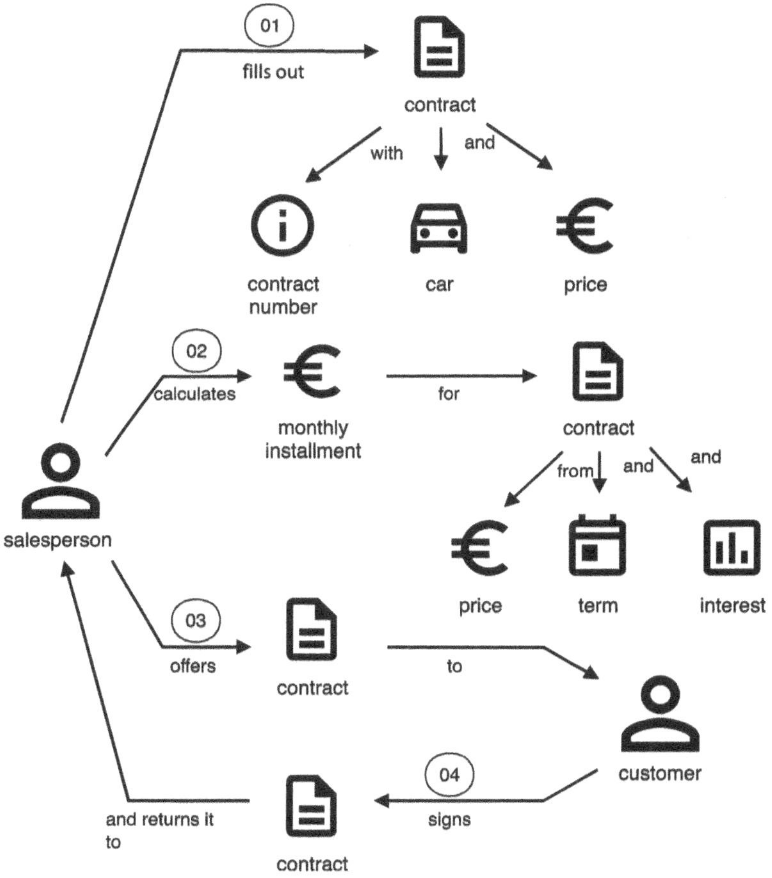

Figure 11.5 *Alphorn 6: Offering, happy path—FINE-GRAINED*

Developer Denise: "You said if the customer agrees with the terms of the contract, they will sign it; what happens if they don't agree?"

Salesperson Sandy: "They reject it, usually because the monthly installment is higher than they can afford. I then recalculate the contract with a longer lease term. The resulting monthly installment will be lower."

Denise: "I'm going to model this as another story. I'll start with a copy of the happy path. I will remove step 4 and replace it with 'Customer rejects contract.' Also, I will add a step 5, 'Salesperson recalculates with different term.'"

Figure 11.6 shows the second FINE-GRAINED domain story.

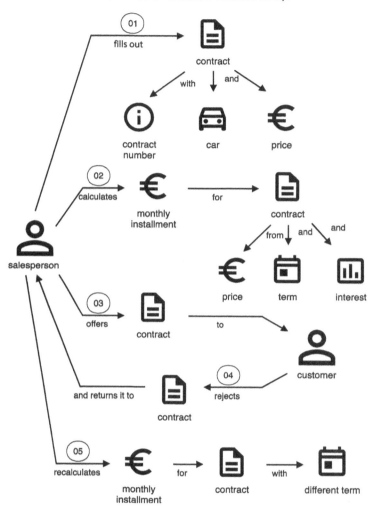

Figure 11.6 *Alphorn 7: Offering, rejection—FINE-GRAINED*

Other variations are considered as well. For brevity's sake we will omit them.

The last steps of the workshop with Denise, Dave, and Sandy are to derive more detailed requirements from the domain stories and to map them to the backbone. For that, we bring up the team's user story map. The sentences in the more FINE-GRAINED domain stories lead to more fine-grained user stories. They are put on a second sequence of sticky notes, below the existing user stories they refine (see Figure 11.7).

Figure 11.7 *Backbone for offering context*

At an even more fine-grained level, the team adds user stories for different variations of the process. Finally, they come to a first product backlog for the "offering" context (see Figure 11.8).

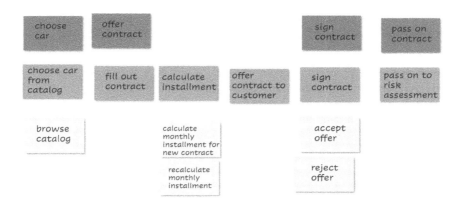

Figure 11.8 *Product backlog for bounded context "offering"*

The team's user story map contains requirements at different levels of detail. Note that the map shows only the names of the user stories—the actual story is written either on the back of the index card (if a physical whiteboard is used for mapping) or in a software tool. For example, here is the description for the user story "recalculate monthly installment":

> *As a salesperson, **I want** to recalculate the monthly installment with changed parameters **so that** I can offer alternative contracts to my customers.*

Adapt the Recipe

So far, we've described a basic recipe for working with requirements. Of course, you can (and should) adapt the recipe. As you have seen, we do that too. Besides the already mentioned "ingredients," the following are worth considering:

- If you find examples for business rules or "decision points" in the annotations, then *Example Mapping* can be the right tool to dig deeper. From there, FINE-GRAINED requirements with acceptance criteria and *BDD scenarios* can emerge. (See Chapter 7, "Relationship to Other Modeling Methods.")

- As an overview of actors and use cases, a UML *use case diagram* (see Chapter 3, "Scenario-Based Modeling") can help.

- A written *use case* is a more elaborate alternative to user stories (again, see Chapter 7).

Limitations

This is not a book on requirements engineering, so we can't cover everything there is to say about this important topic. But since we have written so much about talking to domain experts and users, we should also mention that there are limitations to this approach.

Don't just blindly model what the domain experts tell you!

Domain experts are usually biased, especially when it comes to designing TO-BE processes. These are some limiting factors that we have come across:

- Organizational structures and reward systems.

- Domain experts may know little about technological innovations and the potential of modern software systems (and that's OK because it is not their job).

- The domain experts' vision is limited by what they know, i.e., the current processes and software systems. Hence, they tend to overlook possibilities to reinvent business processes. Small improvements to an existing process are more likely as an outcome than a significantly changed process.

An observation made by John Ferguson Smart addresses premature solutions:

> While users are happy to talk about solutions that they think will fix their problems, they rarely talk about the underlying problems they are trying to fix. After all, if users could always explain exactly what they needed, we wouldn't need disciplines such as Product Management and Requirements Analysis. [Smart 2017]

Smart goes on to say that what domain experts and users ask for is not what they get; and what they get is not what they need.

Also, consider this quote from the originator of DDD, Eric Evans:

> Developers get the experts to describe a desired feature and then they go build it. They show the experts the result and ask what to do next. [...] but if programmers are not interested in the domain, they learn only what the application should do, not the principles behind it. Useful software can be built that way, but the project will never arrive at a point where powerful new features unfold as corollaries to older features. [Evans 2004]

In other words, communication with users is important for building the right software, but understanding the domain to the extent where development teams become (at least in part) domain experts is also crucial to building truly powerful business software.

What to Read Next?

Once your backlog contains requirements at sea level, they should be understood well enough that you can start implementing them. How domain stories can help you do this is the topic of Chapter 12, "Modeling in Code."

Implementing the requirements typically has an impact on how the company does its work. Chapter 13, "Supporting Organizational Change," will show you how to deal with that.

Chapter 12

Modeling in Code

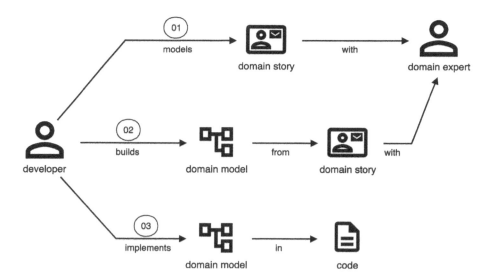

For us, modeling is not reduced to drawing diagrams. If your ultimate goal is to develop software, then, at some point, you need to move from modeling with sticky notes and diagrams to modeling in programming languages. Doing that, you should use terms from the domain directly in your code.

This chapter is for you, if you want to do the following:

- Implement your domain model as object-oriented code

- Implement your domain model as functional code
- Use DDD's tactical design

In this chapter, we will come across some software development terms and concepts that we will explain only briefly. For more details, please see the references provided. In particular, we recommend the following prior knowledge:

- This is the only chapter that contains source code. To make the best of it, you should be able to read code. We will show examples in *Java* and *F#*.
- Building blocks for tactical DDD: *entity*, *value object*, etc. [Evans 2004].
- Practices and technologies from test-driven development/Behavior-Driven Development: *unit test*, *acceptance test* [Beck 2000], *JUnit*, and *Gherkin* [SmartBear 2019].
- Familiarity with UML *class diagram* and *state diagram* [Fowler 2004].

Henning's Tax Accounting Story

I was working with a client that offers an off-the-shelf accounting software solution for small- and medium-sized companies in Germany. The system had been around for three decades and was based on technology in C++. When tax laws changed, the system had to be adapted. The company took this as an opportunity to redesign parts of the system using DDD. As a first step, we sketched COARSE-GRAINED domain stories on a whiteboard. From those we extracted a good context map.

One team built the bounded context dealing with the taxation aspects of sending employees abroad. Since German tax law is notoriously complex, we had to delve deep into the subject. (One literally has to deal with words like "Versendungsabwesenheitsantrag.")

The accounting software company had in-house experts for that subject matter, because it also sends employees abroad. In a two-day workshop with these experts and the developers from the team, we modeled about five FINE-GRAINED domain stories. Each domain story described one specific case of the bounded context's business process.

Since the technology and programming language were a given, we decided to model the domain with object-oriented means, using the DDD building blocks. For every important work object I asked the team the questions "Is this a thing or a value?" or "Does it have an identity?" to separate entities and value objects. Then I asked "Which work objects should be stored together (in the to-be-built system)?" to find the aggregate boundaries and repositories.

> For example, we derived an entity Versendung (which roughly translates to "foreign work assignment"), a value object Einkommensteuer ("income tax"), a repository for the foreign assignments, and an application service Stelle-Antrag ("file application"). Finally, we implemented a first prototype of the domain model in C++ in a mob programming session.
>
> In the next sprints, we iterated over and over again on domain stories, model, and implementation.

From Domain Stories to Domain Model

Collaborative modeling uncovers a lot of knowledge about a domain. To transform this knowledge into software, it must be condensed in a way that is close to software. A *domain model* is one such condensed form of knowledge. It contains the concepts of a domain: physical or purely conceptual things like "contract," "risk," or "voting result." In Domain Storytelling, we call those work objects (see Chapter 2, "The Pictographic Language").

In addition to these *structural* aspects of a domain, the domain model also describes the *behavior* of the concepts. These are the activities such as "to sign" or "to vote" that tell us what the work objects can do, what can be done with them, and how other work objects can interact with them.

Domain Logic Patterns

Designing a fully-fledged domain model is one of several architectural styles that are used to implement the domain layer[1] of an application. These so-called *domain logic patterns* are listed here:

- *Transaction script*

- *Table module*

- *Anemic domain model*

- *Domain model*

---

1. Layered architecture [Buschmann et al. 1996] was the state of the art when DDD was conceived, and the name *domain layer* dates from that time. In the meantime, the community has learned that the "above/below" distinction of the layered architecture is not sufficient to imagine what we want the architecture to be. That's why today we tend to also use the "inside/outside" distinction. This is expressed in the more elaborate styles *Hexagonal* [Cockburn 2005], *Onion* [Palermo 2008], and *Clean Architecture* [Martin 2018]. Thus, the domain "layer" (like other "layers") we're talking about is actually more of a domain "ring." Since the term "layer" is still the one used throughout the industry, we will stick to it in this chapter.

A certain familiarity with these patterns is not required but can help you understand the rest of this chapter. Good books on this subject are *Patterns of Enterprise Application Architecture* [Fowler 2003c] and *Patterns, Principles, and Practices of Domain-Driven Design* [Millet/Tune 2015].

For every bounded context of a system a different style can be chosen. The style *domain model* is the typical choice for the core domain(s).[2]

When you start writing code without knowing the domain properly, your domain model will most likely be *anemic* [Fowler 2003a]; it will be data-centric with operations to manipulate the data. Let's look at an anemic example from Alphorn: a class LeasingContract with a method setSignatureDate(LocalDate date) (see Figure 12.1).

LeasingContract
signatureDate
getSignatureDate() setSignatureDate()

Figure 12.1 *Don't: Build an anemic domain model*

Although this model may be adequate for a trivial bounded context, it has flaws: The signature date can at all times be set to any value. But in the "offering" bounded context, a contract can be signed only if (a) the installment has been calculated and (b) it has not already been signed. This is a *business rule*, also referred to as a *policy*.

A good domain model prevents programmers (and users) from breaking the rules of the domain.

A strong behavioral model is expressive and reflects the domain. Instead of an anemic pile of variables that change their values, a rich behavioral model ensures integrity and consistency with *invariants*. To achieve that, one must understand what happens in the domain—and look at the *verbs*. These are the right questions to ask:

- What are the users doing to achieve their goals?
- How do users handle the work objects?

---

2. A *core domain* is a bounded context that is essential to a company, i.e., a real business asset [Evans 2004].

- In which way do they manipulate them?
- How do users exchange information and work together?

These are also the questions that a moderator asks in a Domain Storytelling workshop.

Domain stories are a great resource for a domain model because they contain the structural *and* behavioral aspects of a domain. You can distill the domain model from one or several stories (typically a handful). You need the right level of detail, i.e., FINE-GRAINED domain stories at sea to fish level (see Chapter 4, "Scope") that take place within one bounded context (see Chapter 10, "Finding Boundaries"). Maybe you have modeled such domain stories during a requirements workshop (see Chapter 11, "Working with Requirements") and you also have written requirements as input for the domain model.

Now that you know what to distill, the question is, how do you express the domain model? One possible answer is: directly in code! However, sometimes it makes sense to express it in an intermediate format first. Such intermediate formats can be any of the following:

- Behavior-Driven Development (BDD) style scenarios [North 2006]
- Formal modeling languages like UML (usually *class diagrams*) [Fowler 2004]
- Class, responsibilities, collaborators (CRC) cards [Beck/Cunningham 1989]
- Design-level EventStorming [Brandolini 2021]

It is important to understand that the purpose of a domain model is not just to preserve domain knowledge. The purpose of domain *modeling* is to design software that expresses the domain. Getting a design right is an iterative, incremental process. Sometimes, the refinement requires continued coding; sometimes you have to go back to modeling with domain experts. Eric Evans describes this process as a *model exploration whirlpool* [Evans 2016].

Back to the Leasing Example

Let's look at the Alphorn example again. In Chapter 10, "Finding Boundaries," we have modeled the COARSE-GRAINED domain story with bounded contexts Alphorn 1a. We're focusing on the context "offering" now (see Figure 12.2).

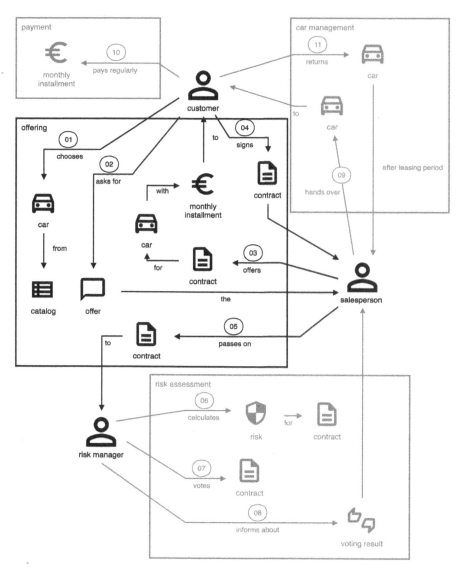

Figure 12.2 *Alphorn 1a: Leasing subdomains, focus on "offering"*

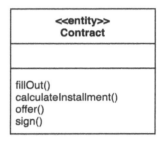

Figure 12.5 *Entity* Contract

Interactions with a contract—like filling out, calculating the installment, and signing—turn into methods (see Figure 12.6).

```
<<entity>>
Contract


fillOut()
calculateInstallment()
offer()
sign()
```

Figure 12.6 *Entity* Contract *with methods*

Figure 12.7 visualizes the general rule of thumb: "work objects turn into classes, activities turn into methods."

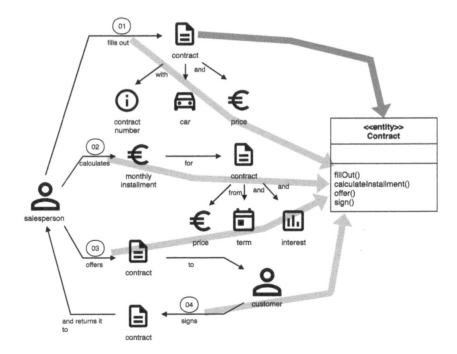

Figure 12.7 *From domain story to class diagram*

Other work objects such as installment, price, term, and interest do not have an identity, so we model them accordingly as *value objects* (see Figure 12.8). In this case, the mentioned types also become parameters of the operation `calculateInstallment()`.

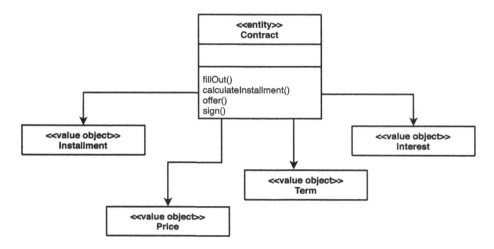

Figure 12.8 *Entity* Contract *with value objects*

When digging deeper into the domain, you will see that all operations have preconditions and can be called only in certain states. Expressing these invariants in your code makes it more readable and robust.

If you use test-driven development [Beck 2000], you start coding the domain model by converting our BDD scenarios into executable acceptance tests. Listing 12.4 shows the first Alphorn BDD scenario again.

Listing 12.4 *Acceptance Test for Alphorn 6, Sentence 2, with Concrete Values*

```
1 Scenario: Calculation of a contract for a midsize car
2   Given a filled out contract
3     And the price is EUR 40000
4     And the term is 48 months
5     And the interest is 3.7 % p.a.
6   When the contract is calculated
7   Then the monthly installment is 897.80 EUR
```

Listing 12.5 shows an implementation as a JUnit test case.

Listing 12.5 *JUnit Implementation of the Acceptance Test for Alphorn 6, Sentence 2*

```
1 import org.junit.jupiter.api.Test;
2 import static org.assertj.core.api.Assertions.assertThat;
3
4 @Test
5 void calculateContractForMidsizeCar() {
6   // given
7   var contract = new Contract(
8     Car.of("Volkswagen ID.3"),
9     Amount.of(40000, Currency.EUR));
10
11   // when
12   contract.calculateInstallmentFor(Term.of(48), Interest.of(3.7));
13
14   // then
15   assertThat(contract.installment())
16     .isEqualTo(Amount.of(897.80, Currency.EUR));
17 }
```

while writing the JUnit test, we have identified two more types: `Currency` and `Amount`. (More on that later.)

To make the test run, we need to implement the classes and methods used in the tests. We present only the signatures of the classes and methods here, so as not to go beyond the scope of this book. We start with the entity[3] `Contract` in Listing 12.6.

Listing 12.6 *Java Implementation of the Entity* `Contract`

```
1 import org.jmolecules.ddd.annotation.Entity;
2
3 @Entity
4 public class Contract {
5
6   public Contract(Car car, Amount price) { /* ... */ }
7
8   public void calculateInstallmentFor(Term term, Interest interest) {
9     /* ... */
10   }
11
12   public Amount installment() { /* ... */ }
13
14 }
```

Then we add the value objects (see Listing 12.7).

---

3. In our examples, we use annotation libraries from xMolecules [xMolecules Website] to mark which DDD building block a domain model class represents. The Java examples facilitate jMolecules.

Listing 12.7 *A Sketch of the Java Implementation of the Value Objets*

```
 1 import org.jmolecules.ddd.annotation.ValueObject;
 2
 3 @ValueObject
 4 public class Car {
 5   public static Car of(String description) { /* ... */ }
 6 }
 7
 8 @ValueObject
 9 public enum Currency { EUR, GBP, USD }
10
11 @ValueObject
12 public class Amount {
13   public static Amount of(int amount, Currency currency) { /* ... */ }
14 }
15
16 @ValueObject
17 public class Term {
18   public static Term of(int numberOfMonths) { /* ... */ }
19 }
20
21 @ValueObject
22 public class Interest {
23   public static Interest of(float interestInPercent) { /* ... */ }
24 }
```

Then, the class Contract is completed with tests for and implementations of the methods offer() and sign() similarly to calculateInstallmentFor() (here omitted for brevity). Interestingly, there is no method fillOut(), although we designed it earlier in the class diagram. Instead, we use the typical Java mechanism for filling out (i.e., creating)—a constructor. This is an example of a programming language influencing the design. There is always a trade-off to be made between (a) expressing the domain in the purest and most "correct" way and (b) not fighting the programming language and writing code that seems "unidiomatic" in that language.

Also, we have not implemented the types Price and Installment sketched earlier (shown in Figure 12.8). Instead, we built a single type Amount because both "price" and "installment" are expressed as an amount of money. So, those work objects became names for variables and parameters instead of types.

Earlier, we learned an important business rule from the domain experts: A contract can be signed only if (a) the installment has been calculated and (b) it has not already been signed. To reason about invariants in the bounded context, it is helpful to visualize the life cycle of a contract as a simple state machine, as in Figure 12.9.

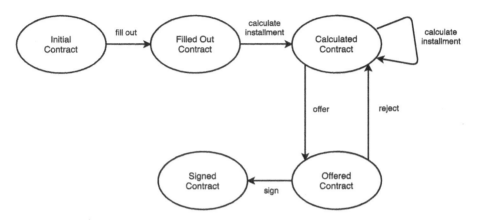

Figure 12.9 *Entity* `Contract` *as state machine*

To express the invariants that we modeled in the state machine, *Design by Contract* (DbC) is a great help [Meyer 1997]. With DbC, method signatures are extended with *pre-* and *postconditions*. Preconditions have to be fulfilled to call the method; postconditions are guaranteed by the method. Unfortunately, DbC is still not supported out of the box in most programming languages (see [Thomas/Hunt 2020]). The Pragmatic Programmers' recommendation (and ours) is to utilize it as a thinking tool nonetheless.

In languages without built-in support for DbC, one can check pre- and postconditions with *assertions* [Evans 2004]. Traditionally, preconditions are defined with the keyword `require` and postconditions with the keyword `ensure`; since Java does not support DbC in the language, we have to emulate it here with the keyword `assert` (see Listing 12.8).

Listing 12.8 *Java Implementation of the Entity* `Contract` *with Assertions*

```
1  import org.jmolecules.ddd.annotation.Entity;
2
3  @Entity
4  public class Contract {
5
6    public Contract(Car car, Amount price) { /* ... */ }
7
8    public boolean isCalculated() { /* ... */ }
9
10   public void calculateInstallmentFor(Term term, Interest interest) {
11     /* ... */
```

```
12     assert isCalculated() // postcondition
13   }
14
15   public Amount installment() {
16     assert isCalculated(); // precondition
17     /* ... */
18   }
19
20   public boolean isSigned() { /* ... */ }
21
22   public void sign() {
23     assert isCalculated(); // precondition
24     assert !isSigned(); // precondition
25     /* ... */
26     assert isSigned(); // postcondition
27   }
28
29 }
```

As you can see, we have introduced a new method `isCalculated()` in Listing 12.8, line 8, that can be used to define the postcondition of `calculateInstallmentFor()` (line 12) and the precondition of `installment()` (line 16). Similarly, we defined the method `isSigned()` (line 20).

From here on, we "just" need to flesh out the implementation.

A Functional, Domain-Driven Implementation

With the means of a functional language, it is possible to express the domain in an elegant way. The work objects that turn into entities and value objects are implemented as *types*. Activities are implemented as *functions*. An implementation of the domain model from earlier in F# might look like in the listings in this section. Let's start with the value objects in Listing 12.9.[4]

Listing 12.9 *F# Implementation of the Value Objects*

```
1 open NMolecules.DDD
2
3 [<ValueObject>]
4 type Car = Description of string
5
6 [<ValueObject>]
7 type Currency =
```

---

4. In the F# examples we make use of nMolecules, the .NET variant of xMolecules [xMolecules Website].

```
 8   | EUR
 9   | GBP
10   | USD
11
12 [<ValueObject>]
13 type Amount =
14   {
15     amountValue: int
16     currency: Currency
17   }
18
19 [<ValueObject>]
20 type Term = NumberOfMonths of int
21
22 [<ValueObject>]
23 type Interest = InterestInPercent of float
```

We implement the entity Contract as the state machine from Figure 12.9. Our goal is to use the type system of the programming language to *make illegal state unrepresentable* [Wlaschin 2018]. We do this by first defining a type for each state, like FilledOutContract and CalculatedContract in Listing 12.10.

Listing 12.10 *F# Types for the States of the* Contract

```
 1 type FilledOutContract =
 2   {
 3     number: ContractNumber
 4     car: Car
 5     price: Amount
 6   }
 7
 8 type CalculatedContract =
 9   {
10     number: ContractNumber
11     car: Car
12     price: Amount
13     term: Term
14     interest: Interest
15     installment: Amount
16   }
17
18 type OfferedContract = (* ... *)
19
20 type SignedContract = (* ... *)
```

To implement `Contract` itself, we use an algebraic data type (see Listing 12.11).

Listing 12.11 F# *Implementation of the Entity* `Contract`

```
1 open NMolecules.DDD
2
3 [<Entity>]
4 type Contract =
5   | FilledOut of FilledOutContract
6   | Calculated of CalculatedContract
7   | Offered of OfferedContract
8   | Signed of SignedContract
```

The activity "The salesperson calculates the installment for the contract" (sentence 2 in Alphorn 6; see Figure 12.3) is implemented as function `CalculateContract` in Listing 12.12.

Listing 12.12 F# *Implementation of* `CalculateContract`

```
1 type CalculateContract =
2   FilledOutContract -> Term -> Interest -> CalculatedContract
3
4   let calculateContract : CalculateContract =
5     fun filledOutContract term interest ->
6       (* ... *)
```

For the sake of brevity, we will not flesh out the implementation.

If you want to dive deeper into the topic of implementing domain models in a functional style, read Scott Wlaschin's excellent book *Domain Modeling Made Functional* [Wlaschin 2018], which has heavily influenced this section.

When a Simpler Style Is Enough

Building a clean, behavior-rich domain model is not always the right choice. The beauty of that design comes at a price. When the price is not justified, building a transaction script, table module, or the like may be appropriate. For example, some parts of a domain may be rather data-centric in nature. In these cases, the behavior is often adequately modeled with create/read/update/delete (CRUD) operations. If this is the case, it does not make sense to invent something that is simply not justified by the domain. CRUD modeling needs not to be bad per se.

Having said that, the more interesting parts of the domain are those that are *not* data-centric. This is typically the case in what DDD calls the *core domain*.

What to Read Next?

Now that we have running code in the domain layer, the next step would be to add the surroundings: application layer, user interface layer, and infrastructure layer. That way we develop it into a whole system. However, this book is not about software architecture. If you are interested in an implementation of the Alphorn example with UI and persistence, take a look at the *LeasingNinja* [LeasingNinja Website]. For further reading on how to integrate a domain model into a sound software architecture, we recommend these books:

- Carola Lilienthal's *Sustainable Software Architecture* [Lilienthal 2019]
- Tom Hombergs's *Get Your Hands Dirty on Clean Architecture* [Hombergs 2019]
- Martin Fowler's *Patterns of Enterprise Application Architecture* [Fowler 2003c]

For more on domain modeling with OO or FP, read the following:

- Bertrand Meyer's *Object-Oriented Software Construction* [Meyer 1997]
- Scott Wlaschin's *Domain Modeling Made Functional* [Wlaschin 2018]

Finally, two books cover domain modeling and architecture from a DDD point of view:

- Vaughn Vernon's *Implementing Domain-Driven Design* [Vernon 2013]
- Scott Millet with Nick Tune's *Patterns, Principles, and Practices of Domain-Driven Design* [Millet/Tune 2015]

We have now arrived at the code level. When the first iteration is done, let's start the next one by learning the language (Chapter 9), checking the boundaries (Chapter 10), and working on requirements (Chapter 11) again.

Also, the implementation will influence how the organization does its work, so it can be interesting to see how to support organizational change (Chapter 13).

Chapter 13

Supporting Organizational Change

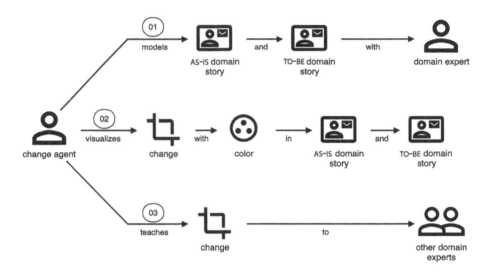

So far, we have looked at different ways that Domain Storytelling helps build software. When this software comes into use, it will influence how people in the company work.

The goal of a new software system is usually to make work easier, faster, more efficient (or in short: better). This goal will not be achieved by digitalizing bad manual processes. Neither will a pile of requirements magically turn into a seamless business workflow. To build good business software, you need to go beyond merely modeling the current situation. You will need to design the future way of working. Domain stories help to do this and visualize how new software will change the way people work.

This chapter is for you, if you want to do any of the following:

- Design how work should be done in the future

- Optimize business processes

- Want to discuss and promote change in business processes

- Have to bring new software into use

- Have to roll out a new version of an existing software

Stefan's State Authority Story

Once, a state authority commissioned us to help them gather requirements for a new software system. The domain involved a lot of legal matters and expert decisions. The domain experts' tasks were not supported by specialized software systems. Basically, they just used typical office software.

There was a big obstacle on their way to better software support: The authority had offices in four cities, and each office had to do the same tasks—but they all did them differently. This meant either they needed a software system that supported a high degree of flexibility or they had to align their business processes. The state authority decided to do the latter.

To design a new way of working, we first looked at how the domain experts worked currently. To get an overview of their tasks, we met with representatives from all offices and mapped their current responsibilities to a UML use case diagram (see Chapter 7, "Relationships to Other Modeling Methods"). Then, we had follow-up workshops where we modeled the use cases as domain stories—office by office. We had at least four domain stories for every use case (one for each office, and some use cases required several stories for us to understand them sufficiently). The scope of these domain stories was FINE-GRAINED (sea level), AS-IS, and DIGITALIZED (even though there was hardly any software involved).

Once we had modeled the different versions of the business processes, we started to compare them and used colors to indicate differences. In a workshop that again included participants from all offices, the differences were discussed, and the domain experts explained to each other why they worked that way. It turned out that many differences were actually negligible. In these cases, deriving a consolidated business process from the existing ones was straightforward. However, if a common process was not obvious, we chose to design one starting with an empty canvas rather than basing it on an existing one.

When the domain experts returned to their offices, they found it easy to explain to their colleagues what was discussed in the meetings. They just needed to compare the AS-IS and TO-BE domain stories for each use case to understand how their work would be affected by the change.

Changing People's Workflows

During the average employee's career, the way their work is done will usually change several times. The reasons for this change may be manifold: because new tasks are to be done, because the company is re-organized, or because the process is optimized.

Modeling the Change

Change is always hard—hard to understand and hard to achieve. In *More Fearless Change*, Mary Lynn Manns and Linda Rising point out that *head, heart, and hand* have to be addressed equally by the change agent [Manns/Rising 2015]. When bringing change to an organization, it is important for everybody to understand the following:

- What changes
- Why it changes
- How it affects me
- How I can help

Domain stories can help by visualizing what will be different in the future (and what stays the same):

- Because of change in the work itself

  - Caused by process optimization

  - Caused by legal obligations

- Because of the introduction of a new software system

To make the change between the processes visible, it often helps to modify the domain stories by coloring the symbols. Figure 13.1 shows a typical legend for such domain stories. Removed or changed elements are red in the e-book or light gray in the print version of this book. New or changed elements are green (e-book) or dark gray (print). Elements that do not change stay black.

Figure 13.1 *Visualizing change—a typical legend*

The resulting stories visualize the output of a discussion, but they don't carry all the explanations. Hence, you should at least write down the key decisions and the rationale behind them, either as an annotation or in a separate document.

Back to the Leasing Example

In the Alphorn auto leasing case study (see Chapter 8), we modeled the risk assessment process with Raymond the risk manager. In doing this, he recognized that the process was suboptimal. Since the team did not want to just digitalize a bad process, the as-is story Alphorn 3 (see Figure 8.3) was developed further into the to-be story Alphorn 4 (see Figure 8.4). The latter shows the optimized process.

He now wants to visualize what is changing from a business point of view. Therefore, he compares the two PURE domain stories. To make the change between the processes visible, the team modifies the domain stories by coloring the symbols according to the legend from Figure 13.1. The results of this modification are the AS-IS story Alphorn 3a (see Figure 13.2) and the TO-BE story Alphorn 4a (see Figure 13.3).

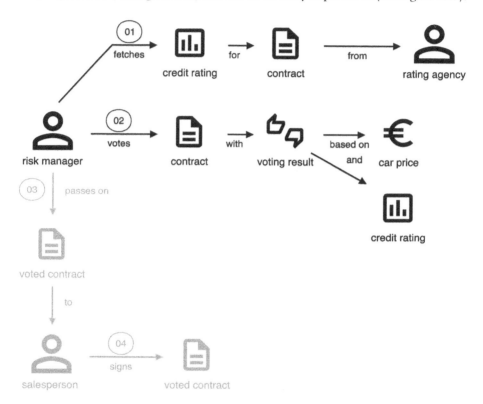

Figure 13.2 *Alphorn 3a: Risk assessment—FINE-GRAINED, PURE, AS-IS—colored*

When the two domain stories are side by side, it is easy to spot the difference. This makes it easy to *explain* the difference, too.

In the collaborative modeling sessions that led to the previous stories, not all risk managers were present. Raymond can now use the stories to explain the new process to the other risk managers.

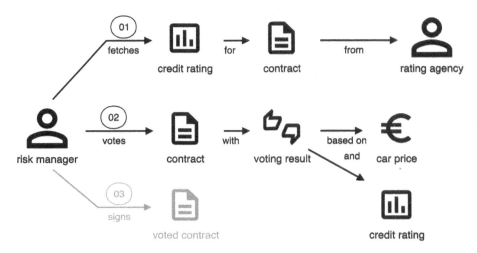

Figure 13.3 *Alphorn 4a: Risk assessment—FINE-GRAINED, PURE, TO-BE—colored*

Every member of the risk management team can see the following:

- This icon represents me.

- The red/light gray arrows connected to that icon show which tasks will change for me.

- The green/dark gray arrows connected to that icon show what will be new for me.

Using the domain stories Alphorn 3a (see Figure 13.2) and Alphorn 4a (see Figure 13.3), Raymond explains: "The management has decided: You don't have to pass on the voted contract (step 3) anymore; you just sign the contract yourself."

As we have seen, using color can help highlight changes. An alternative to colors is to use groups: one group to show what is changing and one group to show what stays the same. In our experience, this is not as helpful as using colors. This is mainly because the different parts in the story that change cannot easily be grouped. Also, readability can suffer. However, for simple domain stories like Alphorn 3 and Alphorn 4, grouping changes can be a viable option, as you can see in Figures 13.4 and 13.5.

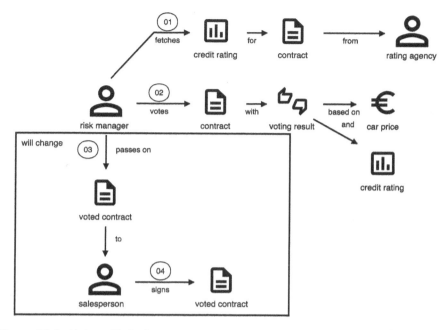

Figure 13.4 *Alphorn 3b: Risk assessment—FINE-GRAINED, PURE, AS-IS—grouped*

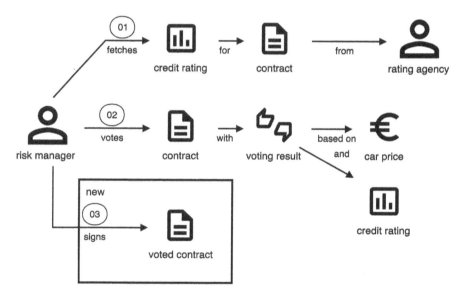

Figure 13.5 *Alphorn 4b: Risk assessment—FINE-GRAINED, PURE, TO-BE—grouped*

Digitalizing Work

Another reason for changing a process is because of the introduction of a new software system.

Designing Viable, Software-Supported Processes

To-be processes played an important role in Chapter 11, "Working with Requirements." There, we advised you to not just blindly model what your users tell you. We discussed the limitations to a collaborative design process: Domain experts often find it difficult to imagine software solutions other than the ones they are familiar with. They also do not know what is possible with modern technology. Other limiting factors include organizational structures and reward systems. In our experience, many domain experts favor small improvements over significantly changed processes.

Back to the Leasing Example

When we started working with Alphorn, they had a somewhat old-fashioned, in many parts paper-based, way of operating their business. When the new online leasing service is introduced, it will change the daily work of its users, both because they will now use software instead of the old system and because the process itself will be a bit different.

Alphorn 2 describes how the work is done today (see Figure 8.2). Alphorn 5 contains the to-be-built system (see Figure 8.5). With the latter, the team explored how the system will influence the business process. Both stories are now colored to visualize the changes. Figures 13.6 and 13.7 show the result.

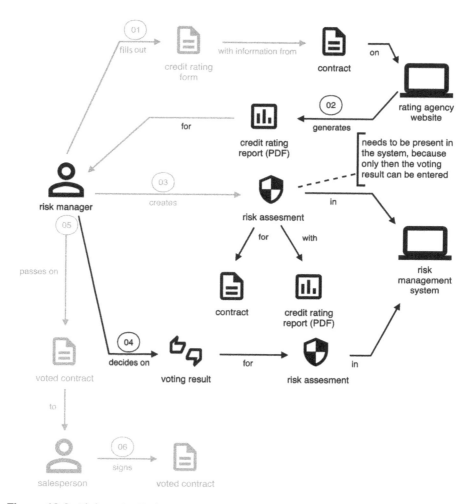

Figure 13.6 *Alphorn 2a: Risk assessment—FINE-GRAINED, DIGITALIZED, AS-IS—colored*

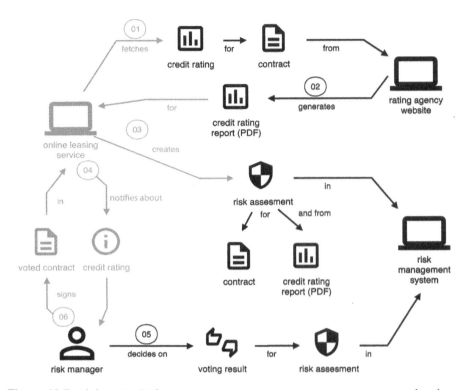

Figure 13.7   *Alphorn 5a: Risk assessment—FINE-GRAINED, DIGITALIZED, TO-BE—colored*

The members of the risk management team can see the following:

- This icon represents me.

- The red arrows show which tasks will change for me or will be done by the system in the future.

- The green arrows show what will be new for me.

Raymond explains the new process with the help of domain stories: "You will not have to fill out the credit rating form (step 1 in Figure 13.6) or create a risk assessment (step 3) anymore; this will be done automatically by the new online leasing service. It will notify you when a credit rating has arrived. Then you decide the voting result in the same way that you always have (step 5). Finally, you have to sign the voted contract in the new online leasing service."

Putting AS-IS and TO-BE situations side by side highlights what will be different with the new system. The people designing the process can see if their ideas can work, and the people who will use the new system can see how their work is affected.

What to Read Next?

Organizational change is interwoven with other topics covered in this book:

- Designing TO-BE processes will uncover requirements for new software systems. That's why organizational change and working with requirements (see Chapter 11) often go hand in hand.

- Also, organizational change can move domain and team boundaries around. In Chapter 10, we described an analytical way of finding boundaries for software systems and teams. However, boundaries cannot only be identified, they can be *designed* by changing the communication structure of an organization. That means you can make use of Conway's Law [Conway 1968] to design communication structures to promote your desired software architecture (the so-called *inverse Conway maneuver*).

Chapter 14

Deciding Make or Buy and Choosing Off-the-Shelf Software

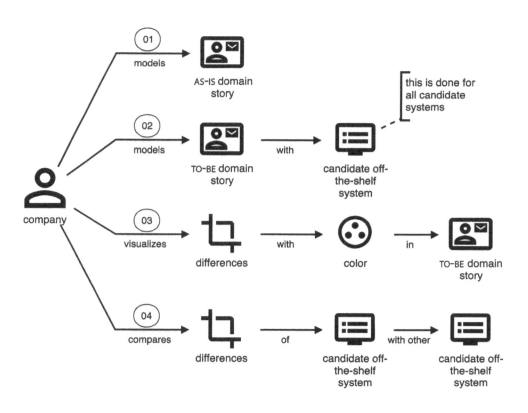

Not every piece of software is custom-built. Many domains are supported by off-the-shelf software. Domain stories can help you to decide whether a new software system should be developed or bought. Often, this decision is the logical next step after identifying bounded contexts, like we did in Chapter 10, "Finding Boundaries." For every bounded context,[1] you should ask yourself: Do we build this part of the software ourselves, or do we buy an off-the-shelf solution? "Buy" is used in a broad sense here and can also mean to use open-source software.

If the decision is to buy an existing solution, usually several vendors will offer their products. Here, too, domain stories can be useful in making a choice.

This chapter is for you, if you want to do any of the following:

- Compare different solutions and find out which is the best for your situation

- Make pros and cons of standard software visual

Stefan's Insurance Story

When an insurance company decided to acquire a new software system for customer relationship management (CRM), they asked me to help them with the selection process. One important constraint was that the new CRM system had to be off-the-shelf software. Company guidelines required at least three comparable offers from suitable vendors. To achieve that, the company followed a multistage process:

1. Research the market to identify about ten possible vendors.

2. Give those vendors equal access to a requirements document and ask them for offers.

3. Compare the offers using a weighted decision matrix.

4. Invite the top three vendors to give a demo to sales representatives (the future users of the system) and other stakeholders.

5. Evaluate the demos and factor the results in the decision matrix to make the final decision.

---

1. In reality, off-the-shelf solutions usually make sense only for so-called *generic subdomains*, a term from the DDD literature; see, for example, *Implementing Domain-Driven Design* [Vernon 2013].

I had worked with the insurance company before to analyze their IT landscape. We had modeled many AS-IS, DIGITALIZED domain stories then, including those relevant to a CRM system. For selecting the new CRM system, we used domain stories for steps 2 and 4 of the selection process.

The requirements document was largely comprised of functional requirements (of course, it also described technical constraints and quality requirements, but those are not relevant to this story). We used several sources to come up with functional requirements: features that the old CRM system had, features we discovered during market research, and features the sales representatives considered useful. However, we did not provide only a list of functional requirements. We also provided domain stories that we had modeled with sales representatives and other stakeholders. The stories showed how they wanted to use the system and how it would integrate with existing software systems.

The scope of the domain stories was TO-BE and rather FINE-GRAINED (about sea level). We chose to tell DIGITALIZED stories (with software systems). That allowed us to express our expectations, for example:

- That the document management system should notify the CRM system if customers send or receive letters

- That changes to contracts in the host system need to be reflected in the CRM system

- That interactions between the customers and the telephone customer support need to be documented in the CRM system

When we asked vendors for their offers, we made clear that the domain stories were suggestions. We asked them to clarify if the processes we had described could be realized with their software or if they had suggestions that would improve the processes. The answers that the vendors gave us were useful for determining how much customization would be necessary for a system. For every process, we could ask ourselves: Do we pay to customize the CRM system so it fits the intended process? Or should we instead change the intended process to fit the CRM system?

To help the vendors understand the domain stories, we did not provide just the pictures; we provided a textual description, similar to a use case (see Chapter 7, "Relationship to Other Modeling Methods"). After all, we could not talk to vendors directly until step 4 of the process, the demo.

In the fourth step, the domain stories played another role: We asked the vendors to prepare a demo that reenacted the most important domain stories. This made it easier for the stakeholders to compare the demos because all three vendors followed the same "screenplay." The survey after the demos resulted in a clear ranking of vendors. Ultimately, the vendor that won the demo round also had the highest overall score and won the contract.

Understand the Processes of Off-the-Shelf Solutions

When buying a software, you have to choose between the offered solutions. Make an educated decision by modeling the process with the different solutions.

Back to the Leasing Example

In Chapter 10, "Finding Boundaries," we found the bounded contexts for Alphorn. For the context "offering," the IT department is working on implementing their own solution (see Chapter 11 and Chapter 12). Now, for the "payment" context, Harold, the head of IT, considers purchasing an off-the-shelf product. (See Figure 14.1.)

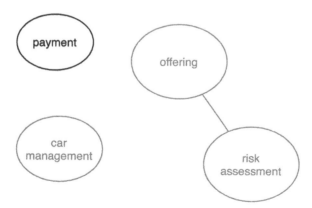

Figure 14.1 *Context map for Alphorn, focus on "payment"*

Harold wants to compare the different solutions that are offered in the market: the two competitors *Paynator* and *GreatPay*. He asks us for support.

As a first step, we meet with Amin, the domain expert from the accounting department to model FINE-GRAINED, PURE domain stories for the "payment" context. The stories will help to define what requirements a solution has to fulfill. Two cases are looked at—a successful payment (the standard case; see Figure 14.2) and a missing payment (see Figure 14.3).

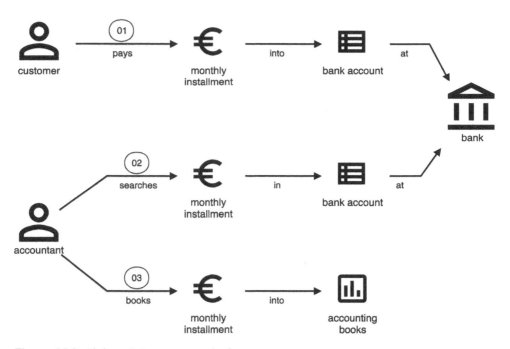

Figure 14.2 *Alphorn 8: Payment, standard case—PURE*

Now that the team understands the PURE process, they look at how the process would change with the different offered systems. Like in Chapter 13, "Supporting Organizational Change," we use color to mark what is new in a process: green in the e-book, dark gray in print.

The team evaluates the Paynator system first (see Figure 14.4).

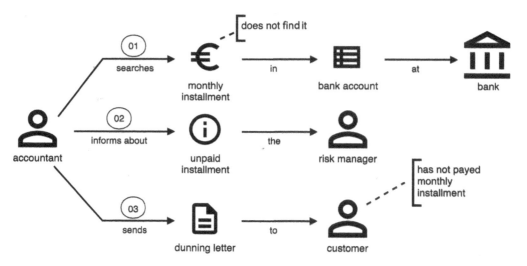

Figure 14.3 *Alphorn 9: Payment, missing payment—PURE*

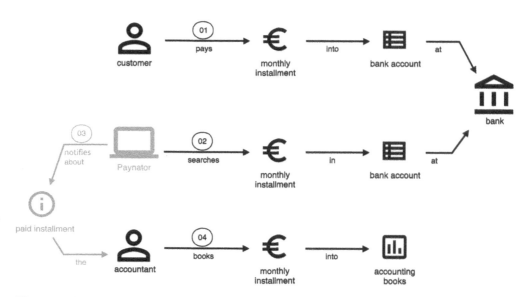

Figure 14.4 *Alphorn 8a: Payment, standard case—DIGITALIZED—with system Paynator*

Raymond: "I compare the car price to the price risk table."

Stefan: "What is the risk price table?"

Raymond: "It calculates the probability of missing payments based on the price of a car."

Stefan: "Could you please explain that?"

Raymond: "Whenever a customer doesn't pay an installment, the accounting department informs us about it."

Stefan: "Ah, I heard something about that when I talked to accounting!"

He brings up Alphorn 9 again (which was written with accountant Amin in Chapter 14, "Deciding Make or Buy and Choosing Off-the-Shelf Software") and points to sentence 2 (see Figure 15.2).

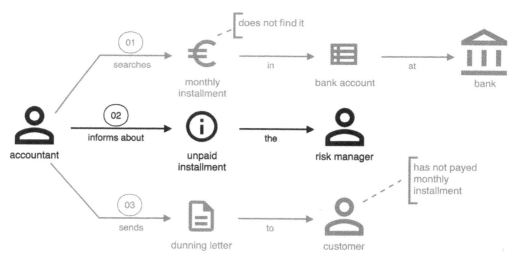

Figure 15.2 *Alphorn 9: Payment, missing payment—*PURE

Raymond: "Precisely! When I hear about the unpaid installment, I enter it into the missing payments tracking. From that, the risk price table is extracted with a VLOOKUP."

Stefan: "Let's put all of this into another domain story...."

Together, they model domain story Alphorn 10, which is shown in Figure 15.3.

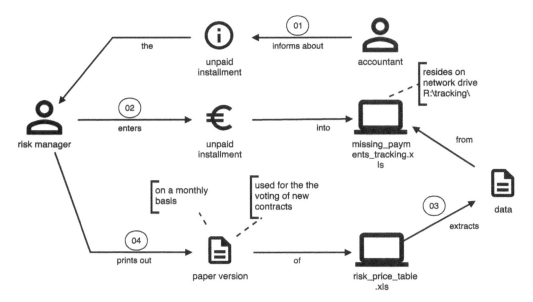

Figure 15.3 *Alphorn 10: Missing payments tracking—DIGITALIZED, AS-IS*

Stefan: "OK, so the missing payments tracking is an Excel sheet! And the risk price table is another one."

Raymond: "Yes, that's true."

So Harold was right: A significant part of business logic (the missing payments tracking) relies on Excel files. The conversation with Raymond continues and covers topics such as the usability and error-proneness of the current software solution. All of this information flows into Harold's IT portfolio management. Harold assesses the operational risk of the Excel files and determines a need for action. Together with the Alphorn 10 domain story, he can now convince Becky that he needs funding to make tracking future-proof.

Hidden use of software systems becomes obvious when work objects appear out of the blue. Either you have domain experts telling you that they "look up the XYZ list" or they answer your question "How do you know that?" with something like

"I got that from the ABC report." When you ask them where the XYZ list and the ABC report come from, you will often discover that software systems like Microsoft Access, Excel, Lotus Notes, or shell scripts are used.

What to Read Next?

The systems that are found in the shadows are part of the overall IT solution. They should at least be visible in the context map (see Chapter 10, "Finding Boundaries").

The shadow systems may be replaced by systems developed by the IT department. Then you will want to work on the requirements (see Chapter 11, "Working with Requirements") and implement them (see Chapter 12, "Modeling in Code").

Chapter 16

Conclusion

Understanding each other will always be challenging. Domain Storytelling (or any other method for that matter) will not make this fact magically go away. But Domain Storytelling can do a lot to mitigate the problem. In fact, we believe that the potential has not yet been fully realized.

The Future of Domain Storytelling

Collaborative modeling is an emerging discipline, and Domain Storytelling is still a relatively new technique. We think the future will bring exciting developments—new methods and new ways to combine other methods with Domain Storytelling.

Tool support is another field where we expect more development. For occasional Domain Storytelling workshops, there are currently already several good solutions. For frequent use, however, there is less choice of tools, with Egon.io providing the best support for the method. We are curious to try new tools. Nonetheless, in many modeling situations, a whiteboard, a marker, and some sticky notes are still all you will need. Let's hope more companies coat their walls with whiteboard paint!

In this book we have described purposes for which we have personally used Domain Storytelling. We've focused on using Domain Storytelling to facilitate software development. However, it can be useful in other fields, too. Some purposes that did not make it into this edition:

- **Workflow automation:** Use Domain Storytelling to learn what to automate. Then, transition to BPMN to make workflows executable.

- **Business process documentation:** Utilize domain stories as a lightweight and easy-to-understand alternative to long written texts or more formal diagrams.

- **Process optimization:** We've only scratched the surface of this topic. Model the current process as an AS-IS domain story. Then, optimize the process and draw it as a TO-BE domain story.

We're sure that the community of Domain Storytelling practitioners will find many more purposes.

The Essence of Domain Storytelling

Whatever the future holds for Domain Storytelling, some aspects will endure because they are the essence of the method:

- **Collaborative:** Several people engage in telling (and listening to) one story, each adding their own knowledge and perspective.

- **Conversational:** It is an interactive form of storytelling—a conversation of storytellers and listeners, who ask questions. The conversation is facilitated by a moderator.

- **Visual:** Talking and listening directly to each other has been, is, and will be the best way for people to communicate. Visualization opens up an additional feedback channel and helps to retain the discussed topics for a long time. Storytelling is also a modeling activity!

- **Scenario-based:** A domain story is about one concrete, meaningful example of a business process.

- **Purposeful:** Domain Storytelling is not an end in itself but a means to reach a goal. The goal can be to improve organizations, to build better software, or to make the work of the domain experts easier, faster, and better.

- **Versatile:** Depending on the goal, the scope of a domain story can vary in granularity, can be about different points in time, and can show software-supported or pure business processes.

- **Integrated:** Domain Storytelling can be combined with techniques from Domain-Driven Design, requirements engineering, testing, agile software development, and other disciplines.

Now, start modeling and have fun! We would love to hear your experience and questions. If you like, share them with us using the hashtag #domainstorytelling or at stefan@domainstorytelling.org and henning@domainstorytelling.org!

Appendix

The History of Domain Storytelling

In the early 1990s, a group of computer scientists[1] at the University of Hamburg began to research techniques for business software development. They realized that it was important for developers to understand the tasks, workflows, and domain language of the future users. For joint workshops, the developers required techniques that would support equal cooperation between the various participants. The graphical means of representation available at that time, such as flow charts and UML diagrams, proved to be unsuitable. Those reinforced the *model monopoly* of the computer scientists in the sense of Stein Bråten [Bråten 1973].

Inspired by Peter Checkland's proposal of a generally understandable diagram technique—called *rich pictures* [Checkland 1975]—the group developed *cooperation pictures* as a technique for engineering requirements. A cooperation picture shows actors and the objects that the actors work with. Actors and objects are visualized as icons and connected with arrows to show joint tasks. The earliest paper in English on this method that we know of is from Anita Krabbel, Sabine Ratuski, and Ingrid Wetzel (later Schirmer) and was published in 1996 [Krabbel et al. 1996]. Figure A.1 shows an image from that paper visualizing the admission of a patient in a hospital.

Cooperation pictures are an ancestor of Domain Storytelling's pictographic language. However, cooperation pictures did not tell a story. They were created in workshops with domain experts, but *after* the domain experts had been interviewed and textual scenarios were written—rather than during the discussion.

---

1. Including Christiane Floyd, Heinz Züllighoven, and Ingrid Wetzel (later Schirmer).

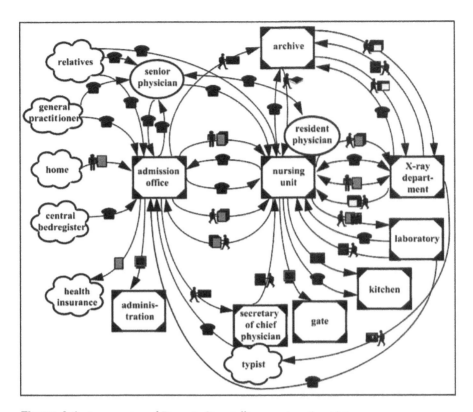

Figure A.1 *An ancestor of Domain Storytelling: cooperation pictures*

The idea for using a visual language for storytelling was born in the year 2000. A car rental company hired a university spin-off that is now known as *WPS – Workplace Solutions Ltd.* to work out some use cases for their business. The employees were familiar with cooperation pictures and knew that visualization techniques can greatly improve workshops. In their workshops, they drew cooperation pictures on whiteboards and added something new: They labeled the arrows with numbers to express a sequence of activities. Now, the pictures had time as a dimension and told stories. After the workshop, they preserved the content of the whiteboard by redrawing the picture on the computer. For lack of a better fitting tool, they used Microsoft PowerPoint. Figure A.2 shows an example of their work.

For documentation, they wrote down the story in prose, referring to the numbers in the picture. They chose this combination of written use cases and cooperation pictures over more formal business process modeling because they had had a great experience in workshops where domain experts had no background in computer science.

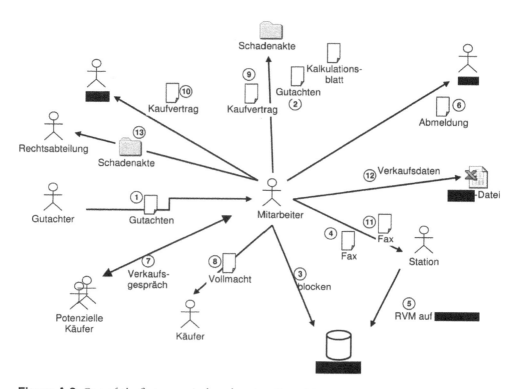

Figure A.2 *One of the first scenario-based cooperation pictures*

The new kind of diagram was initially called *cooperation picture* too and was later renamed *cooperation scenario*. It was a perfect fit for the agile, user-centered, domain-driven style of software development that WPS had been pursuing under the name *Tool and Material Approach* (*T&M*) [Züllighoven 2004]. The founders of WPS, Heinz Züllighoven and Guido Gryczan, had also (and with others) developed that approach. T&M recommends scenarios as a means for communication between domain experts and developers.

Cooperation scenarios were used by WPS employees and others in dozens of software development projects. Many people helped with improving the technique, and by 2003 it had become an enterprise modeling approach with several model types: Cooperation scenarios were augmented with a glossary, use case diagrams, org-charts, process landscapes, and (later) IT landscapes. Enterprise modeling without a proper modeling tool is cumbersome. That's why a modeling solution based on BOC Group's ADONIS was built. Figure A.3 is a picture from the banking domain, created with an early version of the modeling tool.

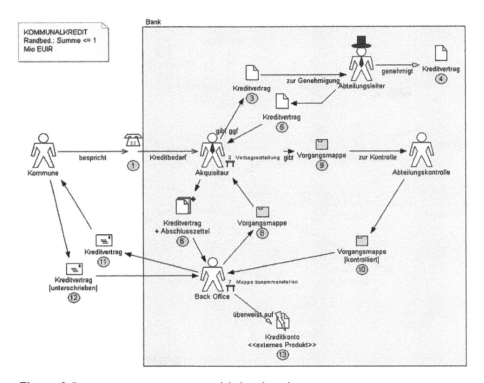

Figure A.3 *A cooperation scenario modeled with tool support*

For the next few years, a method and tool were developed in a kind of co-evolution. They shared a long, German, rather academic name: *exemplarische Geschäftsprozessmodellierung* (*eGPM*), which translates to *exemplary business process modeling* (*eBPM*). eGPM was taught and researched at the University of Hamburg. One of the academic papers of that era is "Design Rationale in Exemplary Business Process Modeling" [Breitling et al. 2006].

The two of us met in 2005, when we both joined WPS. That's also when we met eGPM, which at the time was already our colleagues' favorite method for learning about new domains, having conversations with domain experts, and deriving domain-driven software design. In 2011, a free modeling tool for eGPM was released as part of the University of Vienna's *Open Models Initiative*. Stefan was one of the developers and gradually took over product owner responsibilities.

After Stefan had finished his PhD thesis on modeling enterprise transformation [Hofer 2017], he was approached by Carola Lilienthal, now CEO of WPS. She asked Stefan to take responsibility for the (somewhat dormant) method. Stripping down and renaming the method was the first visible result of this endeavor. In the summer of 2016, Stefan suggested *Domain Storytelling* as a new name for eGPM's cooperation scenario. This new name intentionally resembles *Domain-Driven Design* (*DDD*). Henning, one of WPS's most passionate DDD practitioners, had realized that the ever-increasing DDD community would be the right environment to grow Domain Storytelling.

We started talking and writing about this technique under the name *Domain Storytelling* in 2016. After our talk at the Domain-Driven Design Europe conference in Amsterdam in January 2018, we realized that to become a Domain Storytelling practitioner, you might need guidance that exceeds the format of talks, blogs, and hands-on sessions. Hence, we decided to write this book, which started as a self-publishing project on Leanpub and eventually moved on to become a "real" book at Addison-Wesley.

After presenting the method on DDD eXchange, Explore DDD, and KanDDDinsky, other members of the DDD community started to use and adapt it. It became clear that the different approaches for collaborative modeling have a lot in common. From this insight, the *Visual Collaboration Tools* book [Baas-Schwegler/Rosa 2020] and CoMoCamp [CoMoCamp Website] were conceived. Martin Schimak incorporated Domain Storytelling into *Storystorming* and invented an alternative notation with sticky notes [Schimak 2019]. Nick Tune used it as an inspiration for *Domain Message Flow Modelling* [Tune 2021].

In 2018 the development of an open-source tool was started: Egon.io—The Domain Story Modeler [Egon.io Website].

Meanwhile, Domain Storytelling has also been adopted by the agile, requirements engineering, and Behavior-Driven Development communities. We are looking forward to continuing to write the history of Domain Storytelling!

Glossary

activity—What an actor is doing with a work object. A building block.

actor—A building block that represents a person or software system that plays an active role in a domain story. Actors are the subjects in a domain story's sentences.

annotation—Textual information like a note. Can be about another building block, about a sentence, or about the domain story as a whole.

AS-IS—Point-in-time scope factor of a domain story signifying that the story describes the current situation.

building block—A generic term for the different types of graphical elements used in the Domain Storytelling notation.

COARSE-GRAINED—See *granularity*.

collaborative modeling—The process of bringing developers and domain experts together to share and learn domain knowledge and language.

DIGITALIZED—Scope factor explaining the domain purity. Describes a domain story that contains IT systems, making visible where the business process relies on them.

domain purity—A scope factor that expresses if software systems are part of the domain story. Can be either PURE or DIGITALIZED.

domain story—A picture that represents a scenario told orally by one or several storytellers.

FINE-GRAINED—See *granularity*.

granularity—A scope factor that defines how detailed a domain story is. Can be COARSE-GRAINED (told from a high-level perspective), FINE-GRAINED (told from a low-level perspective with many details), or anything in between, like MEDIUM-GRAINED.

group—Clusters parts of a domain story that somehow belong together. Usually drawn as an outline, e.g., a rectangular shape.

host—The person who invites participants to a Domain Storytelling workshop. Usually has an interest in the outcome of the workshop.

listener—Participant in a Domain Storytelling workshop whose main goal is to gain knowledge. Often a developer.

MEDIUM-GRAINED—See *granularity*.

modeler—The person who draws the domain story in a workshop. Often the same person as the moderator.

modeling canvas—The surface a domain story is drawn on. Doesn't have to be an actual canvas; can be a piece of paper, a whiteboard, or a digital tool.

moderator—The person who leads a Domain Storytelling workshop. Often the same person as the modeler.

point in time—A scope factor that can be either AS-IS or TO-BE.

PURE—Scope factor explaining the domain purity. Describes a domain story that contains no IT systems but only the business process itself.

scenario—One instance of a business process. Tells a concrete story.

scenario-based modeling—A modeling style where different cases of the same process are modeled as different scenarios. Opposed to modeling all cases in one diagram.

scope—The setting of a domain story expressed through the factors granularity, point in time, and domain purity.

sentence—A combination of actors, activities, and work objects. Domain Storytelling's grammar allows for different forms of sentences. The simplest form is *subject* (actor) – *predicate* (activity) – *object* (work object).

sequence number—Notes the order of a sentence in relation to other sentences.

storyteller—Participant in a Domain Storytelling workshop from which other participants can learn about the domain. Often a domain expert.

TO-BE—Point-in-time scope factor of a domain story signifying that the story describes a future situation. Different TO-BE situations are described in different domain stories.

work object—A building block that represents something an actor works on/with. Drawn as an icon that represents the work object itself, a digitalized variant of it, or the medium over which the work object is exchanged.

workshop—A collaborative modeling event to bring together listeners with storytellers. Usually planned by the host and facilitated by a moderator.

Bibliography

You can also find this bibliography at https://www.domainstorytelling.org/book for direct navigation to online resources.

[Adzic 2011] Gojko Adzic. *Specification by Example*. Shelter Island, NY: Manning, 2011.

[Baas-Schwegler/Rosa 2020] Kenny Baas-Schwegler and João Rosa (eds.). *Visual Collaboration Tools*. Self-published, Leanpub, last updated August 7, 2020. https://leanpub.com/visualcollaborationtools.

[Beck 2000] Kent Beck. *Extreme Programming Explained: Embrace Change*. Reading, MA: Addison-Wesley, 2000.

[Beck/Andres 2005] Kent Beck and Cynthia Andres. *Extreme Programming Explained: Embrace Change*. 2nd ed. Boston: Addison-Wesley, 2005.

[Beck/Cunningham 1989] Kent Beck and Ward Cunningham. "A laboratory for teaching object oriented thinking." OOPSLA, 1989. http://www.inf.ufpr.br/andrey/ci221/docs/beckCunningham89.pdf.

[Beck et al. 2001] Kent Beck, Mike Beedle, Arie van Bennekum, Alistair Cockburn, Ward Cunningham, Martin Fowler, James Grenning, Jim Highsmith, Andrew Hunt, Ron Jeffries, Jon Kern, Brian Marick, Robert C. Martin, Steve Mellor, Ken Schwaber, Jeff Sutherland, and Dave Thomas. *Manifesto for Agile Software Development*. 2001. https://agilemanifesto.org.

[Brandolini 2016] Alberto Brandolini. "Optimized for what?" SlideShare, November 20, 2016. https://www.slideshare.net/ziobrando/optimized-for-what.

[Brandolini 2020] ———. "Discovering Bounded Contexts with EventStorming." In *Domain-Driven Design: The First 15 Years* by the DDD Community. Self-published, Leanpub, February 15, 2020. https://leanpub.com/ddd_first_15_years.

[Brandolini 2021] ———. *Introducing EventStorming*. Self-published, Leanpub, last updated February 12, 2021. https://leanpub.com/introducing_eventstorming.

[Bråten 1973] Stein Bråten. "Model Monopoly and Communications: Systems Theoretical Notes on Democratization." *Acta Sociologica* 16, no. 2 (1973).

[Breitling et al. 2006] Holger Breitling, Andreas Kornstädt, and Joachim Sauer. "Design Rationale in Exemplary Business Process Modeling." In *Rationale Management in Software Engineering*, edited by Alen H. Dutoit, Ray McCall, Ivan Mistrik, and Barbara Paech, 191–208. Berlin: Springer, 2006.

[Buschmann et al. 1996] Frank Buschmann, Regine Meunier, Hans Rohnert, Peter Sommerlad, and Michael Stal. *Pattern-Oriented Software Architecture Volume 1: A System of Patterns*. Hoboken, NJ: Wiley, 1996.

[Carroll 2000] John Carroll. *Making Use: Scenario-Based Design of Human-Computer Interactions*. Cambridge, MA: MIT Press, 2000.

[Checkland 1975] Peter Checkland. "The Development of Systems Thinking by Systems Practice—a methodology from an action research program." In *Progress in Cybernetics and Systems Research*, vol. 2, edited by Robert Trappl and Franz Pichler, 278–283. Washington, DC: Hemisphere, 1975.

[Cockburn 2001] Alistair Cockburn. *Writing Effective Use Cases*. Boston: Addison-Wesley, 2001.

[Cockburn 2005] ———. "Hexagonal Architecture." January 4, 2005. https://alistair.cockburn.us/hexagonal-architecture/.

[CockburnOrigin] ———. "Origin of Story Card Is a Promise for a Conversation." http://alistair.cockburn.us/Origin+of+user+story+is+a+promise+for+a+conversation.

[Cohn 2004] Mike Cohn. *User Stories Applied: For Agile Software Development*. Boston: Addison-Wesley, 2004.

[CoMoCamp Website] CoMoCamp—The Collaborative Modeling Unconference. Accessed June 15, 2021. https://comocamp.org/.

[Conway 1968] Melvin E. Conway. "How Do Committees Invent?" *Datamation*, April 1968. https://www.melconway.com/Home/Conways_Law.html.

[Cooper 1999] Alan Cooper. *The Inmates Are Running the Asylum: Why High Tech Products Drive Us Crazy and How to Restore the Sanity*. Indianapolis: Sams, 1999.

[DDDCrew Website] DDD Crew. Accessed May 5, 2021. https://github.com/ddd-crew/.

[DDDHeuristics Website] *DDD Heuristics. Heuristics to share and use for designing software.* https://www.dddheuristics.com.

[DomainStorytelling BookWebsite] Domain Storytelling Book Website. https://domainstorytelling.org/book.

[DomainStorytelling Website] Domain Storytelling Website. https://domainstorytelling.org.

[Egon.io Website] *Egon.io—the Domain Story Modeler.* https://egon.io.

[Egon.io Sources] *Egon.io—the Domain Story Modeler, Source Code.* https://github.com/WPS/domain-story-modeler.

[Evans 2004] Eric Evans. *Domain-Driven Design: Tackling Complexity in the Heart of Software.* Boston: Addison-Wesley, 2004.

[Evans 2016] ———. "Whirlpool Process of Model Exploration." Domain Language. April 2016. https://domainlanguage.com/ddd/whirlpool/.

[Foote/Yoder 1997] Brian Foote and Joseph Yoder. "Big Ball of Mud." *PLoP '97,* Monticello, IL, September 1997. http://www.laputan.org/mud/mud.html.

[Fowler 2003a] Martin Fowler. "Anemic Domain Model." *Bliki.* November 25, 2003. https://www.martinfowler.com/bliki/AnemicDomainModel.html.

[Fowler 2003b] ———. "Multiple Canonical Models." *Bliki.* July 21, 2003. https://martinfowler.com/bliki/MultipleCanonicalModels.html.

[Fowler 2003c] ———. *Patterns of Enterprise Application Architecture.* Boston: Addison-Wesley, 2003.

[Fowler 2004] ———. *UML Distilled: A Brief Guide to the Standard Object Modeling Language.* 3rd ed. Boston: Addison-Wesley, 2004.

[Fowler 2005] ———. "Event Sourcing." *Development of Further Patterns of Enterprise Application Architecture.* December 12, 2005. https://martinfowler.com/eaaDev/EventSourcing.html.

[Freund/Rücker 2019] Jakob Freund, Bernd Rücker. *Real-Life BPMN.* 4th ed. Self-published, 2019.

[Floyd 1992] Christiane Floyd. "Software Development as Reality Construction." In *Software Development and Reality Construction,* edited by Christiane Floyd,

Heinz Züllighoven, Reinhard Budde, and Reinhard Keil-Slawik, 86–100. Berlin: Springer, 1992. http://dx.doi.org/10.1007/978-3-642-76817-0_10.

[Hofer 2017] Stefan Hofer. "Ein Modellierungsansatz für die Umgestaltung von Anwendungslandschaften." PhD diss., University of Hamburg, 2017. https://ediss.sub.uni-hamburg.de/handle/ediss/7180.

[Hofer 2020] ———. "An Introduction to Domain Storytelling." Recorded February 18, 2020. Virtual DDD session. https://virtualddd.com/sessions/19.

[Holtzblatt et al. 2005] Karen Holtzblatt, Jessamyn Burns Wendell, and Shelley Wood. *Rapid Contextual Design*. Amsterdam: Elsevier, 2005.

[Hombergs 2019] Tom Hombergs. *Get Your Hands Dirty on Clean Architecture*. Birmingham: Packt, 2019.

[Hunt/Thomas 2000] Andrew Hunt, David Thomas. *The Pragmatic Programmer: From Journeyman to Master*. Boston: Addison-Wesley, 2000.

[Jacobson 1987] Ivar Jacobson. "Object-Oriented Development in an Industrial Environment." In *OOPSLA '87: Conference Proceedings on Object-Oriented Programming Systems, Languages and Applications*, edited by Norman Meyrow. New York: ACM, 1987.

[Jacobson et al. 2011] Ivar Jacobson, Ian Spence, Kurt Bittner. *Use-Cases 2.0: The Guide to Succeeding with Use Cases*. Ivar Jacobson International, December 2011. https://www.ivarjacobson.com/sites/default/files/field_iji_file/article/use-case_2_0_jan11.pdf.

[Krabbel et al. 1996] Anita Krabbel, Sabine Ratuski, and Ingrid Wetzel. "Requirements Analysis of Joint Tasks in Hospitals." In *Proceedings of the 19th Information Systems Research Seminar in Scandinavia*, edited by Bo Dahlbom et al. Gothenburg Studies in Informatics, Report 8, 733–49, June 1996. https://swa.informatik.uni-hamburg.de/files/veroeffentlichungen/finalIris96.pdf.

[LeasingNinja Website] LeasingNinja. Accessed May 5, 2021. https://www.leasingninja.io.

[LiberatingStructures Website] Liberating Structures. Accessed May 5, 2021. https://www.liberatingstructures.com.

[Lilienthal 2019] Carola Lilienthal. *Sustainable Software Architecture*. Heidelberg: dpunkt, 2019.

[Manns/Rising 2015] Mary Lynn Manns and Linda Rising. *More Fearless Change*. Boston: Addison-Wesley, 2015.

[Martin 2018] Robert C. Martin. *Clean Architecture: A Craftsman's Guide to Software Structure and Design*. Upper Saddle River, NJ: Prentice Hall, 2018.

[Martraire 2019] Cyrille Martraire. *Living Documentation: Continuous Knowledge Sharing by Design*. Boston: Addison-Wesley, 2019.

[MaterialIcons Website] Material Icons. Accessed May 5, 2021. https://material.io/icons/.

[Meyer 1997] Bertrand Meyer. *Object-Oriented Software Construction*. 2nd ed. Upper Saddle River, NJ: Prentice Hall, 1997.

[Millet 2017] Scott Millet. The Anatomy of Domain-Driven Design. Self-published, Leanpub, last updated February 2, 2017. https://leanpub.com/theanatomyofdomain-drivendesign.

[Millet/Tune 2015] Scott Millet and Nick Tune. *Patterns, Principles, and Practices of Domain-Driven Design*. Birmingham: Wrox, 2015.

[Newman 2015] Sam Newman. *Building Microservices: Designing Fine-Grained Systems*. Sebastopol, CA: O'Reilly, 2015.

[North 2006] Dan North. "Introducing BDD." Dan North & Associates. March 2006. https://dannorth.net/introducing-bdd/.

[OMG 2013] Object Management Group. *Business Process Model and Notation*. Version 2.0.2, December 2013. https://www.omg.org/spec/BPMN/

[Palermo 2008] Jeffrey Palermo. "The Onion Architecture." July 28, 2008. https://jeffreypalermo.com/2008/07/the-onion-architecture-part-1/.

[Patton 2014] Jeff Patton. *User Story Mapping*. Sebastopol, CA: O'Reilly, 2014.

[Plöd 2020] Michael Plöd. *Domain-Driven Design by Example*. Self-published, Leanpub, last updated June 24, 2020. https://leanpub.com/ddd-by-example.

[Poupko 2018] Avraham Poupko. "The Importance of Multiple Perspectives When Modeling Software." September 17, 2018. DDD Europe 2018 video. https://laptrinhx.com/the-importance-of-multiple-perspectives-when-modeling-software-avraham-poupko-ddd-europe-2018-543633462/.

[**Rubin 2013**] Kenneth S. Rubin. *Essential Scrum: A Practical Guide to the Most Popular Agile Process*. Boston: Addison-Wesley, 2013.

[**Rumbaugh et al. 2005**] James Rumbaugh, Ivar Jacobson, and Grady Booch. *The Unified Modeling Language Reference Manual*. 2nd ed. Boston: Addison-Wesley, 2005.

[**Schimak 2019**] Martin Schimak. "Storystorming." Medium, June 9, 2019. https://medium.com/plexiti/story-storming-191756f57387.

[**SCS Website**] Self-Contained Systems. Accessed May 5, 2021. https://scs-architecture.org.

[**Smart 2017**] John Ferguson Smart. "When What We Ask for Is Not What We Get, and What We Get Is Not What We Need." *John's Latest Articles* (blog), April 30, 2017. https://johnfergusonsmart.com/how-great-teams-deliver-great-products/.

[**Smart 2019**] ———. "Feature Mapping—a Lightweight Requirements Discovery Practice for Agile Teams." *John's Latest Articles* (blog), November 6, 2019. https://johnfergusonsmart.com/feature-mapping-a-lightweight-requirements-discovery-practice-for-agile-teams.

[**SmartBear 2019**] SmartBear Software. "Gherkin Reference." Last modified 2019. https://cucumber.io/docs/gherkin/reference/.

[**Thomas/Hunt 2020**] David Thomas and Andrew Hunt. The *Pragmatic Programmer: Your Journey to Mastery*. 20th Anniversary Edition. Boston: Addison-Wesley, 2020.

[**Tune 2019a**] Nick Tune. "Sociotechnical Design Variables." *Nick Tune's Strategic Technology Blog*, Medium, May 24, 2019. https://medium.com/nick-tune-tech-strategy-blog/sociotechnical-design-variables-52b7048f7b62.

[**Tune 2019b**] ———. "Modelling Bounded Contexts with the Bounded Context Canvas: A Workshop Recipe." *Nick Tune's Strategic Technology Blog*, Medium, July 22, 2019. https://medium.com/nick-tune-tech-strategy-blog/modelling-bounded-contexts-with-the-bounded-context-design-canvas-a-workshop-recipe-1f123e592ab.

[**Tune 2021**] ———. "Domain Message Flow Modelling." DDD Crew. Latest commit February 4, 2021. https://github.com/ddd-crew/domain-message-flow-modelling.

[**Tune Blog**] ———. *Nick Tune's Strategic Technology Blog*. Medium. https://medium.com/nick-tune-tech-strategy-blog.

[Vernon 2013] Vaughn Vernon. *Implementing Domain-Driven Design*. Boston: Addison-Wesley, 2013.

[Vernon 2016] ———. *Domain-Driven Design Distilled*. Boston: Addison-Wesley, 2016.

[Vernon 2017] ———. *Domain-Driven Design kompakt*. Translated by Carola Lilienthal and Henning Schwentner. Heidelberg: dPunkt, 2017.

[Verraes Blog] Mathias Verraes. *Blog*. http://verraes.net/#blog.

[Wikipedia Cockburn-Style] Wikipedia, "Cockburn-style use cases." https://upload.wikimedia.org/wikipedia/commons/8/82/Cockburnstyle_use_cases.svg.

[Wlaschin 2018] Scott Wlaschin. *Domain Modeling Made Functional*. Raleigh, NC: Pragmatic Bookshelf, 2018.

[Wynne 2015] Matt Wynne. "Introducing Example Mapping." *Cucumber Blog*, December 8, 2015. https://cucumber.io/blog/bdd/example-mapping-introduction/.

[xMolecules Website] xMolecules. Accessed May 5, 2021. https://xmolecules.org/.

[Yong 2017] Ed Yong. "The Desirability of Storytellers." *The Atlantic*, December 5, 2017. https://www.theatlantic.com/science/archive/2017/12/the-origins-of-storytelling/547502/.

[Young 2010] Greg Young. "Command and Query Responsibility Segregation." *CQRS Documents*. November 2010. https://cqrs.files.wordpress.com/2010/11/cqrs_documents.pdf.

[Zuill 2014] Woody Zuill. "Mob Programming – A Whole Team Approach." *Agile 2014*. https://www.agilealliance.org/resources/experience-reports/mob-programming-agile2014/.

[Züllighoven 2004] Heinz Züllighoven. *Object-Oriented Construction Handbook*. Amsterdam: Elsevier, 2004.

Index

X - Y - Z

Photo by Marvent/Shutterstock

VIDEO TRAINING FOR THE **IT PROFESSIONAL**

LEARN QUICKLY
Learn a new technology in just hours. Video training can teach more in less time, and material is generally easier to absorb and remember.

WATCH AND LEARN
Instructors demonstrate concepts so you see technology in action.

TEST YOURSELF
Our Complete Video Courses offer self-assessment quizzes throughout.

CONVENIENT
Most videos are streaming with an option to download lessons for offline viewing.

Learn more, browse our store, and watch free, sample lessons at
informit.com/video

Save 50%* off the list price of video courses with discount code **VIDBOB**

Photo by izusek/gettyimag

Register Your Product at informit.com/register

Access additional benefits and **save 35%** on your next purchase

- Automatically receive a coupon for 35% off your next purchase, valid for 30 days. Look for your code in your InformIT cart or the Manage Codes section of your account page.

- Download available product updates.

- Access bonus material if available.*

- Check the box to hear from us and receive exclusive offers on new editions and related products.

Registration benefits vary by product. Benefits will be listed on your account page under Registered Products.

InformIT.com—The Trusted Technology Learning Source

InformIT is the online home of information technology brands at Pearson, the world's foremost education company. At InformIT.com, you can:

- Shop our books, eBooks, software, and video training
- Take advantage of our special offers and promotions (informit.com/promotions)
- Sign up for special offers and content newsletter (informit.com/newsletters)
- Access thousands of free chapters and video lessons

Connect with InformIT—Visit informit.com/community

Addison-Wesley • Adobe Press • Cisco Press • Microsoft Press • Pearson IT Certification • Que • Sams • Peachpit Press

 Pearson